T0129856

Growing Happiness

Turning Loss and Grief into Joy

LILIBET RAIN

BALBOA.PRESS
A DIVISION OF HAY HOUSE

Balboa Press books may be ordered through booksellers or by contacting:

Balboa Press
A Division of Hay House
1663 Liberty Drive
Bloomington, IN 47403
www.balboapress.com
844-682-1282

Print information available on the last page.

ISBN: 979-8-7652-3224-8 (sc)
ISBN: 979-8-7652-3226-2 (hc)
ISBN: 979-8-7652-3225-5 (e)

Library of Congress Control Number: 2022913952

Balboa Press rev. date: 09/15/2022

To my angel daughter, who has helped me to learn the immense value of forgiveness, gratitude, and love.

I Do Not Forget

I do not forget, sweet yesterdays,
And the fond love through the years.
Drowned in thought, somehow, I find
Myself smiling through my tears.

There were days, my smile was lost,
Moments I didn't know what to do …
There were days of memories
Of sweet yesterdays with you.

You always brought me a song,
That dried the tears I cried,
And made me remember yesterdays
Whose joys have never died.

Though our years together are a memory
Whose yesterdays are past,
I still hold you beautiful and alive
In sweet memory, that time outlast.

—George Sauz

Contents

Preface

Desmond and Mpho Tutu, in their *Book of Forgiving*, said that to heal yourself, you need to tell your story. And the big bonus is that in telling your story and in your healing, you can help others to heal too. I have several stories to tell, so one or more of them may help you in your healing journey. The process of healing entails the development of several useful personal resources, such as the abilities to forgive, to express gratitude on a regular basis, to love unconditionally, and to prioritize our own happiness in life. All of these can be developed if you so choose. However, my hope is that this book goes beyond helping people to heal; I hope that it influences them to look and find their joy, their passion, their driving force—in fact, their reason for being here on this planet.

I see passion as the vehicle to help us travel on a road which may be smooth and straight but is more likely than not full of potholes, bumps, obstacles, and poorly placed signposts. A major diversion or trauma in your life can drive you to look at the map of life much more carefully, and in particular, to make sense of it instead of wandering aimlessly along the highway. And many of us are fortunate enough to have guidance and support from those physically on this planet and even from those who are with us in spirit.

This book is dedicated to my greatest guide and teacher, my angel daughter Isobel, who continues not only to want the best for me but to want me to be happy. She is the soul who is at the centre of my most painful story but whose love has taught me that there is always a reason to go on, regardless of the trials we meet along our journeys. Simply put, we should never give up, as tomorrow is indeed another day full of opportunities to achieve joy.

I have learnt that pain is real, but it increases when we are unable to accept what has happened. You might say that if we are here to experience joy, why do we have to go through such sadness in the first place? This is the yin and yang of life. In your worst despair, there is hope, and there is always, always something to make you grateful. (Being alive, for instance!) In this materialistic world of ours, we take so much for granted, and only when it is taken away are we suddenly aware of its value. As Joni Mitchell sang in "Big Yellow Taxi", "Don't it always seem to go that you don't know what you've got till it's gone?" Wouldn't it be fabulous if we could appreciate what we have right now and do our best to nurture it without going through trauma? But sadly, that is often not the case. By healing from the pain, letting go of the past, and having gratitude for what is and a positive outlook for the future, we hold the keys to having lives of happy moments and, more importantly, of underlying joy.

As a strong believer in the law of attraction, I have struggled with the concept that I could have attracted the various episodes of trauma in my life, but now I understand that behind it all is a way forward, a way to have a greater love for myself and others, to grow spiritually, and to live more joyfully. So I say, bring it on! Ultimately, this is a positive function of being on this planet and not a negative one. When you read of some of the unpleasant experiences that have occurred on my journey through life so far, it may sound unbelievable that I can proclaim that it was all for my own good. But in the words of one of my favourite singers, Kelly Clarkson, "What doesn't kill you makes you stronger!" And a strong person can help others, which, as many spiritual teachers tell us, is exactly why we are here in this space-time dimension.

I have heard some very negative statements from people, such as "The human race is so evil that it should be destroyed," "There are so many terrible things happening in the world," and "Life is bad," but my reaction is to keep calm and accept that it is their belief and not mine. No one else can change your beliefs—only you can do that. Thus, if you decide the world is a good place and look for and appreciate the many acts of kindness and compassion that take place on a daily basis, you will create your own happiness. At the heart of Eckhart Tolle's teaching is the concept that all suffering is in the mind and that your thoughts can make your life very miserable.

Fortunately, the opposite is also true. You have the power to plant seeds (thoughts) which will germinate, grow, and bloom into joy.

Where does the analogy of growing seeds fit in? I believe I found my greatest passion, organic vegetable farming, as a result of my house burning down and me losing almost all my worldly possessions; it was the phoenix that rose out of the fire. Once I connected to this driving force, I not only survived the disaster but thrived! And later on, I found that I was equipped with the power to handle whatever else life could throw at me with grace. When you find your true passion, the creativity just flows. Every day provides new opportunities, and life is wonderful! And working with nature is a great way to connect to the cycle of life, which teaches us that energy is never ending and so is the spirit.

The passion that I have just alluded to is the same one that not only helped me make sense of my life but also of this book! I knew that I wanted to write about how passion and purpose give us the strength and drive to live this life to the fullest with happiness as a constant companion, but I did not know how to set it out in a way that was natural, organic, and flowing. Well, as always, nature had all the answers. I was thinking about seeds one sunny morning, specifically of producing exciting heirloom, non-GMO seeds that would get everyone, especially children, to want to learn about how to sow them and grow them. *Yes,* I thought, *when you have ideas that you are passionate about, you can't wait to plant them. They will then start to thrive and grow because of the care and love you bestow upon them, and the result is joy and happiness.* Thus, in a nutshell, you are "growing happiness". It was one of those magical, spiritual moments that I am now so grateful to say are part of my everyday life.

However, you can't just stick seeds in the ground anywhere and expect them to germinate. Even if by some luck they do, they will quickly wither and die if not provided with the conditions they need. In my workshops and school visits to the farm, I always emphasise that the soil is a living entity that requires nurturing if we are to grow anything successfully. Indeed, without healthy topsoil, we are all doomed. The year 2015 was the International Year of Soils for a very good reason. At the rate at which we are using chemicals in large-scale commercial farming, cutting down trees and even whole forests, and destroying nature in general through urbanisation, we won't have any good topsoil left in thirty years. No good topsoil equals no plants, no insects, no animals and birds, and no us!

In the same way that we need to take care of the soil and prepare it for planting, we need to love ourselves and work on ourselves in order to grow spiritually and find true and lasting happiness. Some soils do not need a great deal of preparation to provide an ideal growing medium, while others need thorough digging and the addition of a lot of organic matter over time. I am an example of the latter type of soil. The first section of this book, "Preparing the Soil", represents the early experiences of my life where a lot of the hard work and preparation for the possibility of future growth took place.

Richard Rohr says that you cannot move on to a higher state without having had trauma in your life. But of course, you would need to have learnt something from that trauma; it is not automatic that you move higher without any effort on your part. Traumas, or life challenges, can be viewed as fairly minor after the dust has died down, although they may appear much greater at the time due to being magnified by emotion. When challenges of a much greater magnitude on the "Richter scale" occur later, these minor incidents may appear to shrink into insignificance. We should not, however, forget that even minor quakes from the distant past can still shape our future lives or that they can also have a cumulative effect, resulting in moments when we say, "Enough is enough!"

The focus of the second and third sections is mostly on my major life challenges, as these, I have come to realise, were my greatest times of growth and were responsible for me sowing the seeds of hope and developing resilience. Looking back, I could be forgiven for wondering why I went through so many trials. One explanation could be that I fell short in the learning department during my previous lifetime. This, I believe, would not have been the result of being a slow learner but of having had a short life experience. (Well, that's the explanation I prefer, anyway!) When I was in my late teens,

I suddenly became aware that I was going through a new stage of life. It was if I had not gotten past fifteen years in my last stint here on earth. That would account for needing to have so many challenging experiences; I did not have a chance to grow very much in my last lifetime.

To say I am grateful for all the new learning experiences in my present life might sound dishonest. I was certainly not very happy at the time they manifested and was thus far from thankful. Two of them in particular were extremely painful emotionally during and after the time they occurred. Indeed, these experiences could have brought me to my knees, and my story could have ended prematurely. But the point—probably the whole point of this book—is that I not only survived but went on to find real joy in my life, and I hope to inspire others to do the same.

In the fourth and final section of this book, "Coming into Bloom", I discuss one remaining major challenge that caught me completely off guard but ultimately led to me being known by my friends as "Eternal Sunshine". Despite all that I had already gone through, the bud had not yet opened. There was one essential missing ingredient needed to enable it to burst open into full bloom. I needed to love myself fully and unconditionally, warts and all.

The intention of *Growing Happiness* is to provide an awareness that everyday happiness is possible. Happiness is available not only as a passing glimpse of that trophy but also as a sustained feeling of well-being and contentment—in other words, *joy*. No matter what challenges you are going through right now, no matter what terrible experiences you have had in the past, no matter what fears and anxieties you have for the future, the only barrier between you and joy … is you! Happiness is a choice we make, a choice to connect to the truth of our souls instead of to the false, exterior world. My greatest wish for you is that you make a lasting commitment to be happy. The prize will surely be a magical, joyful life beyond your wildest dreams. As my most cherished of all inspirational leaders, his Holiness the Dalai Lama (Tenzin Gyatso), simply proclaims, "The very purpose of life is to be happy."

Part One

Preparing the Soil: The Hardest and Most Important Work

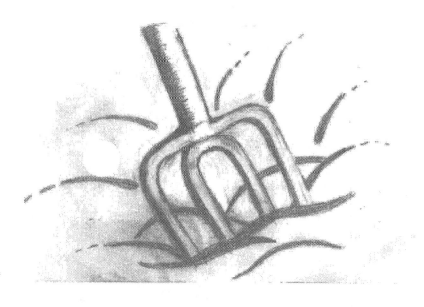

Your only work is to love yourself. Value yourself and embody this truth of self-love and self-worth so that you can be of true service to yourself and those around you.

—Anita Moorjani

The theme of the first section of this book is that a life filled with low self-esteem and a lack of self-love is just like an unprepared vegetable bed; it will require blood, sweat, and tears in order to get it into a reasonable state—one that allows spiritual growth to take place. My major challenges with life-threatening illnesses were a reflection of the disharmony between the way I perceived myself and the reality of what my soul knew me to be: pure, perfect love. As both Anita Moorjani and Mona Lisa Schulz (speaking at the same summit) remind us, everything happens to help us move up to the next level, including illness. As a result of such experiences, you become a different and hopefully more self-loving person who is able to accept your strengths as well as weaknesses.

I used to think that I had somehow attracted the troubles of my younger years as a form of karmic punishment. I thus find reassurance in the new understanding of karma, which is that we create our own experiences for our benefit, not for our destruction. In other words, karma is not a default mechanism that gives us an electric shock for pressing the wrong button. Rather, it is part of the obstacle course we need to travel through to enable us to reach the light at the end of a dark and unhappy tunnel. Becoming aware of the brightness beyond the present situation not only gives us hope for the future but helps us to recognize the fact that we are in a tunnel in the first place and need to get out.

Have you ever wondered how you made it through your early life experiences? It is likely that as teenagers and young adults learning about our roles in the world, we made plenty of mistakes, relying on parents, caregivers, relations, and caring friends to keep us from falling by the wayside. Some of you may have had mentors in the form of religious leaders, real-life heroes and heroines, or inspirational characters from books and movies—all people who were revered for their ability to wade through the muddy waters of life. Others of you may have been blessed with an inner knowing, a GPS based in past life experiences, or were able to connect to guiding spirits or angels. However, many were surely like me: not so fortunate or advanced in spiritual growth at that turbulent time of finding my way into adulthood.

When I look back to those days, I see a naive young woman with self-esteem so low that she had no idea which direction to follow for her own good. My saving grace was that I touched base with my first passion at a young age, about 7 years old. That was when I fell in love with teaching, or to be exact, with the role played my primary school teacher! I remember Mr. Malcom fondly. He was a young teacher who was caring and kind and very patient with his young learners. Without the desire to follow in his footsteps, I think I would have been lost.

Chapter 1

My health status during my early years did not make things easy on me. I managed to contract nearly every known contagious childhood disease during my school years, including German measles and scarlet fever. Fortunately, all of these ailments, even those that were not so common, were diagnosed with ease, and the treatments were equally straightforward. Entering my teenage years, my health story became more mysterious. I was blacking out during school assemblies and suffering from palpitations in the middle of sports activities. I was assured that this was all part of growing up and having those unpredictable hormones. Then again, I was quite competitive in all areas of my schooling, probably needing to prove my self-worth, and had an inclination toward overextending myself. In particular, in netball and hockey matches, I would run frantically up and down the pitch, out of breath and with a pounding heart. That in itself would not have been a problem except that my heart would not stop pounding for some time after leaving the pitch. Eventually, I would recover and return to the game but without the same unabated enthusiasm.

As the years went by, the palpitation episodes not only continued but steadily got worse instead of disappearing once my hormones started behaving themselves. On one occasion, they decided to stay the whole night! I was in my midteens. I had taken on a babysitting job on New Year's Eve, but I had also been invited to a fancy-dress party. I'd known that my parents would not allow me to join in the fun when the clock struck midnight, so my plan was to pretend that I was babysitting into the early hours of the morning, even though I would be released from my duties long before midnight. Of course, I felt excited at the prospect of the party but also guilty about my plan to deceive my parents.

As the time approached for the couple to return, I began changing into my "naughty schoolgirl" outfit (which was quite appropriate, really). I did not get very far, however, as my heart began to beat rapidly. Before I could attempt to put it into reverse, my heart was locked in a high gear. I slowly acceded to putting my own clothes back on, and when the couple arrived, I simply asked them to drop me home. They actually had no idea of my original plan and did not know that my heart was pounding away, and neither did my parents. So, I entered our house and went quickly and quietly to my bedroom, hoping that once I was safely at home and resting, my heart would respond accordingly and the palpitations would come to a welcome end.

I woke the next morning feeling totally drained and knowing that something was very wrong. My heart was still beating nineteen to the dozen. I was very weak, and I had no choice but to involve my parents. At first, I called to my mother meekly from my bedroom. The plea got louder and louder until she finally heard me and came running to my bed. Mum immediately called the family doctor, but it was New Year's Day, so his surgery was not yet open. The receptionist said he would be there at 10.00 a.m. I looked at the clock on my bedroom wall with horror—it was only 8.00 a.m.! How was I going to survive another two hours of this agony?

This was probably the first time I actually listened to my intuition, or inner voice. I decided that if I was going to suffer, then I might as well listen to my favourite album, which was Queen's *Sheer Heart Attack*. It may well be considered a rather inappropriate or unwise choice, but I had received the album as a Christmas present, and there was song on it that I loved called "Misfire". As I eagerly anticipated the start of the song, something miraculous happened. My palpitations just disappeared as quickly as they had first arrived. I was extremely tired but oh so relieved that my torture had come to an end seemingly by itself.

Now that I am aware that there are no coincidences in life, that everything happens according to the universal law of synchronicity, it all makes perfect sense. There was a clear reason for the onset of my galloping palpitations, as well as the fact that anticipating "Misfire" brought them to a grinding halt, and I did not need to be Detective Clouseau to work out that the album title was surely a major clue.

Despite there being a happy ending to this particular episode, the palpitations worsened over the years. As a result, I had to drop out of high-impact exercise, such as dance aerobics, for a fear of an attack. I knew that anxiety was a major trigger, but instead of dealing with that negative emotion, I resorted to either avoidance tactics or the numbing effects of alcohol. However, there were some occasions where the alcohol had the reverse effect and got me overexcited, setting off a chain reaction that led to my heart turning into a runaway train whose brakes were non-existent. Fortunately, I had found a few tricks that brought my heart under control. Sipping very cold water or lying on a cold stone floor seemed to slow down my heartbeat. These tricks, however, lost their effectiveness as time went on.

One evening when I was in my early forties, my second husband-to-be, Stuart, and I went out for supper at a well-known Indian restaurant, which boasted authentic Indian food. I love the spices and flavour combinations found in Indian dishes, although I find some of them rather rich due to the high fat content. I must have consumed more than my stomach could handle, as I felt very uncomfortable by the time I went to bed that night. I was unable to fall asleep, and I had an impending sense of something brewing in my body. Sure enough, around 2.00 a.m., I had to rush to the bathroom. As soon as I would return to the bedroom, I would have to turn tail and go back again for another episode. I was vomiting and having diarrhoea alternatively for over an hour. I eventually just stayed put in the bathroom, hoping that the evacuation of my stomach contents would soon be over. As if that was not bad enough, palpitations took the opportunity to jump into the fray.

I had avoided involving Stuart, as I'd expected my stomach to settle down by itself, but now that palpitations had taken hold, it was another story. I was very weak. I tried all the tricks I had up my sleeve to bring the rapid heartbeat to a halt, but they refused to cooperate. Around 4 a.m., I gently woke Stuart and asked him to take me to hospital; I had had enough. We arrived at the private hospital only to find that the emergency room was under renovation. We were directed to a makeshift emergency room. The nurses quickly diagnosed my condition as a self-inflicted anxiety attack and tried their level best to convince me that all I needed to do was to calm down and relax. (I would like to see them doing that with a hammer pounding inside their chests!) That was, until they took my blood pressure and saw that it barely registered on the scale. A drip was then shuttled speedily to my side containing a solution designed to slow down my heart rate so that it could start pumping normally and send oxygen through my body. Well, that was the idea at least. The problem was that the very low blood pressure which had triggered action from the medical staff also stopped them from achieving it. Every time they tried to insert the needle into a vein, it simply collapsed. The nurse tried my left arm first, because I am left-handed, and then tried my right arm, my legs, and my feet, all to no avail.

At this point, I started drifting out of consciousness into a state of sublime, painless peace. I could see my hands turning blue, but I was totally undisturbed by this phenomenon. Nothing mattered anymore—that was, until I got a glimpse of Stuart on the other side of screen. Stuart looked very anxious. (Later he told me that he was thinking, *What will I do if I lose Lily?*) I could also see the medics preparing the machine which is used restart hearts that have stopped. I had always thought that the use of a defibrillator in "Casualty" and other similar television series looked very dramatic, but I was not at all concerned. However, I was affected by the look of fear on Stuart's face and felt a strong pull and need to stay a while longer on earth. It was then that, as a last resort after seven other attempts, the needle was stuck into a vein in my neck. The life-giving liquid sped down the racetrack directly to my heart. Within seconds, the pounding subsided to a normal pace, and the blood began returning to my hands and the rest of my body. It was an amazing near-death experience, one that was going to help me immensely much later on in my life.

After a day or so in intensive care, the doctor who was allocated to take charge of my recovery declared that I was not getting any younger and that my heart condition would only continue to get worse if nothing was done about it medically. Till then, I had been unaware that any such action was required; after all, I'd been told I was supposed to grow out of the palpitation attacks. Dr Van Wyk's test results, however, revealed that I had a faulty heart valve which sometimes did not close properly when under stress. The valve needed to be repaired by a heart specialist. He recommended that I visit Dr Gratton at Milpark Hospital in Johannesburg, as he was a reputable expert in this field of medicine.

At Milpark Hospital a few weeks later, I met the white-haired doctor, and he carried out an investigation into my heart problem. Under local anaesthetic, a probe was inserted into my groin and was skilfully guided upward until it arrived at its destination—inside my heart! I was given the scary privilege of seeing this for myself on the monitor. Quite fascinating! After the procedure, Dr Gratton confirmed that this condition could not be left untreated I would require catheter ablation in order to burn/remove the tissue that was causing the arrhythmia. He had done this procedure many times before—almost 200—so I was fairly confident that I was safe in his hands.

Some weeks later, I was booked into Milpark for the operation and a day or two of recovery. Standard protocol required me to sign a document giving Dr Gratton permission to insert a pacemaker into my chest in the unlikely event that the ablation was not successful. This could be done while I was still under the effect of anaesthesia without scheduling another operation. Dr Gratton also asked for my verbal agreement to have a group of trainee heart specialists observe the proceedings, and again I agreed. The anaesthetic was meant to last six hours—the procedure was clearly not a simple one—but I started coming round while Dr Gratton and the trainees were still in the theatre. I couldn't hear the words spoken, but it appeared they were discussing what had transpired during the marathon surgery, and from the tone of their conservation, I got a distinct feeling that all was not well.

Waiting for Dr Gratton to finally deliver the outcome of the operation was quite stressful. He did not arrive at my bedside until 3 p.m. the next day, but somehow, I already knew what he was going to say. When he gently broke the news that my operation was one of only two instances in which he had not succeeded in dealing with the faulty valve, I was not surprised. However, I was very fortunate that Dr Gratton had decided not to carry out the pacemaker implant, a decision that has made me eternally grateful to him. Dr Gratton's reasoning was based on the fact that I was quite young (in my early forties) to receive an artificial mechanism to keep my heart regulated and also that the alternative of using medication had not yet been tried.

What Dr Gratton had done, whether he knew the significance of his decision or not, was put the ball back into my court. At the time, I did not understand how much influence we have over our own health or indeed that stress is the main cause of *dis-ease* (disease). Up until then, I'd been a "victim" of life and had just dealt with the consequences of what "happened" to me. I was just a pawn in the game of life, and clearly, I was not a very good player. However, this life-changing event gave me a real need and urgency to develop the confidence I needed to take control of my emotions. It was very clear that letting them get the better of me was no longer an option.

Chapter 2

The "soil preparation" I needed in my early life was not restricted to the area of health. I managed to make quite a mess of my relationships in those early years too. When you have a low opinion of yourself—about the way you look, your popularity, your intelligence, and so on—you tend to be content with second (third, fourth …) best. However, I am not saying that all my relationships were like that. I spent some time with some very kind-hearted young men, but these more positive relationships were destined not to last for very long—mostly because I could not recognise a good thing when it stared me directly in my face.

Why did this happen? I think that those who lack self-love slip easily into partnerships which are at the best unhealthy and at worse life-threatening. I am not proud to tell you that I found myself involved with a married man at one point during my midtwenties. We were both teachers at the same school in Thamaga. I was apparently invisible to his close friend (another teacher), who I desperately loved, and Thero was the second-best option. It worked well in the beginning, because Thero was a friendly, fun guy and we enjoyed being together. I was also blissfully unaware that he was married! By the time I found out, it was already too late for me to back out (or so I thought), as I was hooked. I had grown to love Thero and was unwilling to set myself free from him. I even felt that his wife was the intruder, as she had been living far away from us, although she had slowly but surely gotten herself transferred nearer and nearer to where her husband was working. Thero also assured me that their marriage was over and that he wanted to spend his life with little naive me.

What started off as a tricky situation became like "living life on the edge of a razor", a lyric from a popular song at the time. The dangerous nature of our relationship seemed to strengthen our need to be together, while being apart fed a growing mistrust, so much so that Thero became obsessive about my movements and acquaintances. I became a victim of his jealous rages with scratches around my neck as evidence. Mind you, I can't blame him, as I didn't exactly value my physical well-being either. Throwing myself out of a moving car, even if it was only going five kilometres an hour, is not showing much self-love. But this was all part of how my low self-esteem expressed itself.

Fortunately, just when this destructive relationship was sucking me into a downward spiral, a knight in shining armour appeared on the scene. Musa, a young agriculture teacher, was posted to our school. After a few weeks at Sediri Secondary, this knight charged in and rescued me with a statement that came out of the blue and was so foreign to my ears. Musa arrived at the netball court, where I was coaching, and announced that he loved me and that he could not stand the way I was being treated by Thero. Someone actually loved me! And he was not just anyone. Musa was a handsome and charming young man, admired by his colleagues and students alike. What I didn't know at this time was that he thrived on this admiration.

Breaking free from Thero was not an easy task, especially as he lived around the corner. His wife had moved in with him by this time, but this did not deter his efforts to continue our relationship. Thero completely refused to accept that we could no longer see each other under the circumstances and used every opportunity to mock Musa, who was now on crutches due to a football injury. I really did not want anything to do with Thero anymore, but as mentioned earlier, he was unreasonable and obsessive.

One morning, Thero walked straight into my house (we did not lock our doors in those days in Botswana) to confront me about Musa. I could not believe that he would have the audacity to barge into my home like that with his wife just a few houses away. But she was not at their house. She had followed him and was marching up my path! While I was busy arguing with Thero and trying to get him to leave, I had my back to my open front door. The next thing I knew, a heavy object came crashing down on my skull. I spun round to see Thero's wife with a heavy wooden sculpture in her hand. I screamed at both of them to get the hell out of my house!

It was only after they left that I noticed drips of blood on my dressing gown. I put my hand into my hair, and it came out covered in blood. I ran to my neighbour's house, and they were shocked to see the state I was in. However, they very quickly cleaned me up and calmed me down. I managed to get away with not getting stitches—after all, how I was going to explain the head injury at the local clinic? At least that was the end of the drama in my life for the time being.

My relationship with Musa was considerably more tranquil on the surface. Little did I know what was going on behind my back. To be honest there were plenty of clues. There was the time a young girl came to Musa's house to collect her handbag from Musa's house. Another time, another young woman claiming to be his girlfriend confronted me at a disco. There was a female student at the school who was continually in his presence. There were times when Musa would disappear somewhere. And so on, and so on. But as they say, love is blind, and I badly wanted to believe that I had found someone who really loved me at last.

You will not be surprised, therefore, to find out that my first marriage did not last very long—barely five years. When I finally made the decision to separate from Musa and slowly retreat from our marriage, I felt a big weight being lifted from my shoulders. However, the decision was not based on my unhappiness, as I still had a long way to go toward improving my self-esteem and sense of self-worth. Musa had been far from the ideal partner, but I'd put up with his lack of attention because at least he loved me. I think I would have continued to carry that albatross around my neck if it were not for the intervention of my 5-year-old daughter, Isobel, or Bella, as she is affectionately known.

Musa and I lived apart, as we had been posted to schools in different regions for most of our marriage. Our two girls stayed with me, so it was expected that he would join us at weekends. One Friday evening, when my so-called husband failed to turn up to spend the weekend with his family, I could not hold back the tears. I was unable to get any communication from him, and I felt rejected and unloved until Bella put her arm around me and gently said, "Mummy, I don't want you to cry anymore." I suddenly realised that accepting this unhappy state of affairs was not just about my feelings. It was also hurting my darling daughter—and that I was not going to stand for!

With that weight lifted, my life started to feel lighter and happier. And being in a more positive state, I attracted someone who had a love for his child equal to that I had for mine. We were brought together by a cupid by the name of Vanessa, a dear American friend. She was convinced that her friend and her hairdresser could have a long-lasting relationship with each other far exceeding their previous marriages. It was not love at first sight, but by the second hair appointment, neither of us wanted to let the persistent cupid down. So, I accepted an invite from Stuart and his son for dinner at their house, and the rest, as they say, is history.

Another health problem appeared shortly after starting my relationship with Stuart. We had only been together five months when I was diagnosed with stage 3 cancer of the cervix. Ironically, this only came to light because I got tested for HIV and agreed to have a Pap smear at the same time. I was very worried about the HIV result and was thus relieved to be given all the clear only to find out that I actually had cancer!

The doctors presented me with two choices: either have a biopsy, a minor operation, to investigate the extent of the cancer and then have a hysterectomy only if deemed necessary, or alternatively, resort to the hysterectomy regardless of how far the cancer had spread. The former meant the possibility of two operations and a lot of weeks away from Gaborone High School, where I was teaching art and fashion and fabrics. The latter would only require one operation and a maximum of five to six weeks away from my job. As a couple, we decided that having three children between us from our previous marriages meant that we already had a decent-sized family, and if we were to have a child together, it could cause disharmony amongst the existing children.

In October 1993, I had my womb removed, and to this day, I don't know if the removal was really necessary or not. At that time, apparently, doctors did not divulge to patients what they had found during the operation, so I don't know how far the cancer had actually spread. I guess it makes sense, as after all, you can't put the womb back. Maybe there was a reason why I should not have had any more children. I had always wanted three anyway, and my two girls and Stuart's son added up to exactly that number. I recovered quickly from the operation through my own determination to get back to being independent and back to my students at school. While in hospital, I was even asked by the nurses to give encouragement to other patients, especially a young lady who refused to get out of bed due to the pain of moving around. Movement was an integral part of the healing process and was necessary for avoiding complications. She did not respond well to the advice she was given and ended up needing further treatment, having to stay even longer in pain.

This particular health challenge, looking back, was of less consequence than my heart condition and other challenges to come. I did not suffer any great loss (apart from my womb) and it didn't really have any lasting negative impact on my life as far as I am aware. Everything pretty well returned to normal after a few months. Stuart and I had three young children to take care of, and after a few more years together, we had a wedding to organise.

This sounds like this it should have been the end of the digging and turning of the soil of my life and should have been my way forward to a happy ending, but I am afraid this is far from the truth. The biggest challenges in my life were yet to come. However, a lot of the initial work had been done, and by removing the stones and unwanted material from the soil, I had achieved more clarity. The cobwebs of ignorance had been removed. In the words of another one of my heroes, Mahatma Gandhi, "The truth is by nature self-evident. As soon as you remove the cobwebs of ignorance that surround it, it shines clear."

Part Two

Planting the Seeds of Hope: An Opportunity to Grow through a Positive, Nurturing Attitude

People inherently love nature. Gardening is not complex. It is the connection to the simplest of joys—working with the soil. You plant the seed, you nurture it, you hope it will grow vibrant, turning into something beautiful, something you can share with the world. Growing and nurturing our hopes and dreams is one of the greatest joys in life.

—Oprah Winfrey

The roller coaster ride of my first forty years or so on this planet, although very scary on the downward sections, at least brought me to the realisation that if I dealt with my fear and anxiety, the ride would be much more comfortable and may even be enjoyable. In particular, the near-death experience that resulted in me discovering my heart condition gave me no choice but to work on myself unless I wanted a one-way ticket out of the fairground of life. That was a ticket I was not ready to take. I loved my two daughters very much. I loved my husband-to-be and my stepson too, not to mention my dearest mother, who had gone through so much herself and did not deserve to have the extra burden of worrying about her only daughter.

Preparing the soil had indeed been a lot of work; I made many mistakes and had much to learn. Now I needed to plant healthy seeds in order to benefit from what I had experienced during that time. These seeds would give me hope for a happier and more stable future. It was not the end of the self-work; it was the start. I was open to gaining insight into how to keep my wild emotions under control, push forward with my passion of teaching, and do something purposeful in the world. And with this new found motivation, I would need to nurture myself like never before or else face the stark consequences.

By 1999, I had moved up in my career and now had the responsibility of heading a school, which was something I did not take lightly at all. It had been a source of great joy for me to work with secondary-school children in government schools and then at tertiary level with trainee teachers at the Moshupa College of Education. But now I was leading a group of the most dedicated workers on earth: primary school teachers! I took my role of guiding and counselling the teachers on my team very seriously, and that demanded that I be a strong and healthy role model. This again required inner work to be done.

Secondly, the fact that I had been given the opportunity to choose how I dealt with my heart condition was empowering. I could either rely on medication and possibly have a pacemaker fitted if things got really bad or find ways to improve my self-love, self-esteem, self-value, self-worth, or whatever you would like to call it. Yes, it would be hard work and would require dedication and commitment, but the benefits promised to go far beyond keeping my heart condition under control. I am not sure if I was really aware of those benefits at that time, but I certainly was when my life started to blossom later on.

Chapter 3

As another decade was coming to a close, I was surprisingly excited about turning 50 years of age. I could put all the fumbling around of the last half-century behind me. Surely all of the mistakes and mishaps had laid the foundation for a solid and stable life in my remaining years on the planet. My sense of self-worth appeared to have increased. You can hardly be a head teacher for ten years, in charge of thirty or more teachers and hundreds of children, and not possess a substantial amount of confidence in your value as a person and as a leader. Away from the school setting it was a different story. I still had plenty of self-doubt lurking inside of me. However, I was in a good financial position which made life easy to navigate. My salary and gratuity, along with large lump sums arriving in my account courtesy of all the textbooks I had written by that time, meant that I was able to provide very well for my family. We regularly went on bush trips and beach holidays and visited relatives in the UK. I also furnished the house with every kind of electronic gadget, decorated it with copious sparkling ornaments, and planted a garden of my dreams.

It was not a big deal that my ex-husband did not contribute to our children's education, as I was in a position to ensure that they went to very good private schools in South Africa, including paying for their boarding fees and allowances without help from anyone. My eldest daughter was a very ambitious and hard-working girl and won a scholarship for being one of the top three students at Montle English Medium Primary School. I was working for the owners of both that school and its sister school, Gaborone Private High School, and my children were entitled to free education at both schools, but Bella won free secondary education at the high school solely on her own merit. She was not, however, destined to stay there long. After she was awarded first place in seven subjects in the prize-giving ceremony at the end of her first year at that school, it was clear that Bella had the potential to reach an even higher bar. Indeed, Bella felt that she was not being challenged enough at the high school and was getting bored. Bella also wanted to study speech and drama, which were not taught at any secondary school in Botswana. We finally selected a school for her in Pretoria, South Africa, that was rated as one of the top schools offering private education in that country: St Mary's Diocesan School for Girls. Thus, my daughter went from having a completely free secondary education to joining one of the most expensive schools available. I could afford it, and she deserved it!

Thandiwe, the younger of my two daughters, moved from Montle English Medium Primary School to the South African education system even before completing her final primary year. She chose to attend St Michael's School for Girls in Bloemfontein. That was partly because her step-brother was already at the all-boys St Andrew's School in the same town—the two schools were related—but also because Tandy understood that having two children at St Mary's DSG would have been a financial strain for her mother. From a young age, she was very like my own mother, humble and caring, not wanting to rock the boat if she could help it.

As I approached my 50-year milestone in 2007, I was well equipped in the material-possession department, owning a four-hectare plot, a spacious three-bedroom wood home, another smaller house that I was renting out, a three-litre Mercedes Benz, a Toyota RAV4 for running around in, several wardrobes full of clothing, cupboards full of all sorts of "useful" things, and as I mentioned before, ornaments galore! Both my parents had sadly passed away by this time, and my savings together with the inheritance I received from them had helped me purchase the plot, build our wonderful house, connect electricity, and drill a deep borehole for our water supply, as well as contract builders to put up a lapa (an open building with a thatched roof) on stilts on the rocks at the back of the plot.

I was blessed with not only two wonderful daughters, a supportive and loyal husband, and a sweet stepson, but also an ever-increasing circle of good friends. Although some people may claim that you can only have a few "real" friends, I can safely say that I had many, because they are still close to me today. By nature, I have always been a very friendly person, and spending quality time with like-minded people was high on my daily to-do list. It is not surprising that most of these friends, male and female, were teaching colleagues who I had worked with at a range of education levels. By this time, I had taught at the primary, secondary, and tertiary levels with only preschool left as unknown territory.

The "seeds of hope" mentioned in the title of this section have nothing to do with my material possessions, my family and friends, or even the seeds I was planting in my huge flower garden and modest vegetable patch. I still needed to deal with my anxiety, which hung over me like a black cloud that could drench me in a downpour at any given moment. The anxiety was twined together with an underlying lack of self-worth, which refused to dissolve despite any happiness gained from outside myself. As eloquently stated in *A Course in Miracles*, "You have little faith in yourself because you are unwilling to accept the fact that perfect love is in you, and so you seek without for what you cannot find within." Thus, the seeds of hope were those glimmers of my shining diamond deep within, that perfect love that I had failed to acknowledge. They were my attempts to start loving the "real me" and to connect with my inner knowing, my intuition from my soul. These were the seeds, the beginnings of having self-love and achieving a state of inner joy—no matter what was taking place around me.

Chapter 4

Although I just proclaimed that the literal sowing of seeds in my vegetable patch had nothing to do with the meaning behind this section, that is not entirely true.

My mother, Sylvia, loved to potter around in her garden. Even when a major stroke in her mid-seventies put my mum into a full-care nursing home, viewing beautiful flowers still brought a smile of joy to her face. Thus, it is not surprising that gardening became one of my hobbies too. I actually had many hobbies, as I could never sit still for long without creating something, whether from clay, string, food, fabric, paper, paint, recycled materials, or seeds. When I was much younger, my father had noted that I also created quite a mess, as evidenced by the sewing threads left all over the carpet after I had stitched some masterpiece.

When I arrived in Botswana in 1982, I was posted to a beautiful village called Manyana. It has massive, sculptured rocks and boulders which contrast starkly with the bare sand and thatched homesteads at their feet. The secondary school where I was to teach was very new, and I was expected to help the first group of home economics students to get through their form-three final examinations, practical and theory, despite not having had a teacher for over two terms. My accommodation was a standard teacher's quarters, a semi-detached house with a completely empty yard. The climate was very different from that of the country I had come from; it was dry and hot for most of the year, while England was the opposite. But I was not going to let that dampen my enthusiasm for gardening. By trial and error, I managed to get some flowers to not only germinate but also survive the harsh growing conditions. Unfortunately, barely four months later, I was transferred to another village, and I had to leave behind a thriving flower garden that would be at the mercy of the next occupant of that house.

It was then 1983, and I was 25 years old. From that time onward, I've been on a mission to create a garden wherever I've lived. While working for the government of Botswana, I was moved several times on promotion, and each time, I left a flowering legacy. This did not change when I eventually left the ministry of education's employ to join the private sector. One of these gardening projects came as a result of me becoming the head teacher of Montle Primary School; I was allocated a large house with an equally large (empty) area of land around it. Although, as in all previous homes I had lived in, my stay on the property would be temporary, that did not stop me putting my heart and soul into developing a garden from nothing. This time I went as far as making a few vegetable beds to bring fresh, home-grown green delights into my kitchen. Even though I was no longer teaching home economics, cooking was still one of my favourite pastimes. There is nothing like picking your own vegetables and herbs to create healthy and wholesome food for the family.

My timeline for working at any one place apparently demanded that I move on after five years. I'd spent half a decade at Sediri Secondary School and another half-decade at the Moshupa College of Education. My time as head of Montle Primary School was no different. What was different, however, was that I was finally in a position to buy my own land and later build the house of my dreams on it. And more importantly, I could cultivate the garden of my dreams knowing that this time I would be able to enjoy the fruits of my labour for many years to come.

The piece of land I acquired was a massive four hectares. It wasn't that I was looking for such a huge space in which to live. Rather, that was the size of the agricultural plots on Franklin Road at the far end of Ruretse. What attracted my husband and me to the plot was that it was fairly flat and there were a good number of indigenous trees. However, its biggest attraction was that there was water beneath it, though we did not know how much water at that time. The plot had been surveyed, and the survey indicated that there was an underground stream or two. Fortunately for us, Stuart possessed that rare and very useful talent of being able to divine water, so he also investigated the water situation using two metal rods, which crossed each other wherever water was detected below. Stuart got a very strong reading in the same place as the survey, so we were confident that we definitely had water.

The first development on the plot was not actually part of any plan. There is a large rock outcrop at the back left-hand corner of the plot which somehow caught the attention of some Zimbabwean builders. They proposed that it would be an ideal place to build a lapa on stilts, which they just happened to be equipped to build for the modest sum of 30,000 pula, including all building materials and labour. This sounded like a good idea and a fair deal, so hands were shaken, and the lapa was built.

Initially Stuart, Tandy, and I did not stay on the plot. Bella was already boarding at St Mary's DSG by then, and Stuart's son was not living with us either, as he was at St Andrew's, a boarding school eight hundred kilometres away in Bloemfontein. I was still the head teacher at Montle Primary School at the start of the new millennium, and Tandy was in standard five at the same school. Stuart got the ball rolling with building our dream house by supervising the construction of a "floating" foundation, which we had to use due to the nature of clay soil that constituted most of the plot. The only areas that were not heavy clay were the rocky outcrop already mentioned and a section of sandy loam behind where the house was being built.

At the end of 2002, I resigned from Montle Primary School to start the exciting project of being the manager of my own school! The school would provide quality education in the village of Moshupa. I had been approached by an enthusiastic Motswana woman, Geraldine Pule, who was impressed by the creativity on show at the Montle Primary schoolhouse and my principled work ethic at the school. One day, out of the blue, Gerry presented me with the irresistible offer to manage the school that she was planning to build in her home village. I would be free to run the school however I saw fit—another dream come true! Gerry and her husband took out the loan for the school building and thus would be its owners, while Gerry and I were to be fifty-fifty partners in the business itself.

Leaving employment at Montle Private Primary School meant abandoning an established garden, but it was a small price to pay. And after all, my next garden would be permanent at last. The only snag was that we had not yet built a house on the plot, so we found ourselves camping in tents for several months. A company aptly named Crafty Creations had started the construction of their prototype wood-panel house on our land, but it was far from finished at that time. Previously, they had built dog kennels, guard huts, and garden sheds, so this was a slightly larger and more complicated project for them. However, the fact that we were being guinea pigs meant that the cost of the project was very reasonable. Plus the house would be totally original, and we would have plenty of input in its design.

Our first form of accommodation on the plot consisted of three tents—one for Stuart and me, one for Tandy, and another for clothes and other necessities. Poor Tandy had to wash in a bucket and get dressed in her tent before being taken to school every weekday morning. At least Stuart had left hairdressing by that time and was working at the vegetable farm next to the huge chicken farm in the middle of Ruretse. The school in Moshupa was still being built, and I went there regularly to check on its progress. Thus, during 2003, both my home and my new workplace were taking shape, and apart from being involved with both of them, I spent quite a lot of time getting the garden started. This was done before the borehole construction and water system was completed, so water had to be shipped in from town in twenty-five-litre containers. My main task with the garden, then, was irrigating the plants I had salvaged from my previous home. When we finally moved out of our house at Montle Primary School, there were eight truckloads of plants, garden tools, and accessories and just three loads of our furniture and belongings!

Our life was far from dull with every day bringing new challenges concerning juggling the building projects, gardening, getting Tandy to school on time, and dealing with routine tasks, such as cooking and ironing. The lapa turned out to be a welcome place of refuge, as

I could retreat to this sanctuary to get away from the noise and chaos in the centre of the plot. I did this not to rest but to continue writing my home economics textbooks for Longman Publishing. Power had already been connected in the lapa, enabling me to use my laptop for working on the current manuscript. I am not sure how many books had been published by then, but to date, I have been involved in the publication of over twenty textbooks on home economics, art, and environmental science, either as a contributing author or, in the case of the secondary school Home Economics books, the sole author.

By this point, the royalties for the books had grown in leaps and bounds over the years. Although many hundreds of hours went into giving birth to each manuscript, when the royalties finally appeared in my bank account, it felt like a gift from the Universe. Two hundred pula became two thousand pula and eventually two hundred thousand pula! Thus, not being formally employed for a whole year did not stop me from providing for my family.

Both my dream house and my dream school were gradually taking shape. Stuart assisted the builders to make sure the wooden beauty was everything we wanted it to be: a house with an open floor plan that made it so I could be busy in the kitchen and yet still talk to whoever was in the dining room or watch television in the sitting room beyond it. The entire house consisted of pre-cut panels and tongue-in-groove pine cladding except for the roof, which was painted corrugated iron. Meanwhile, Greenfields English Medium Primary School, far away in Moshupa, was being constructed from cement blocks and face brick, making it look almost too beautiful to be a school.

Chapter 5

We finally moved into the house in May 2003. It was not strictly finished, but it had passed the local occupancy regulations. So, being on the brink of winter's cold fingers, we were given the go ahead. This, of course, made daily life ten times easier than it had been the previous months. My daughters, Tandy and Bella, had their own rooms for the first time, for a start. There was also plenty of space to accommodate Darren, Stuart's son, whenever he visited. Bella was away during the school term and home every school holiday. Darren was at boarding school in Bloemfontein but stayed either with his mother in Durban or with us during his holidays. Tandy was the only child living in the new house full time—a welcome change from a tent!

The house was definitely the most spacious place I had ever occupied. That was just as well, as we had acquired a huge display cabinet, which was the length of the dining room, as well as our extensive assortment of Camp Hill pine furniture. At Camp Hill the disabled trainees always produced quality products and we were happy to be able to support the centre. The cabinet had been given to us by very good friends who were leaving the country to return to their home in Canada. It was of a much darker wood than the rest of our furniture, but that did not matter, as it had lots of shelves on which to show off our many ornaments. It even had cupboards along the bottom to store those artefacts which were not in favour at the time. Despite the vastness of the cabinet, I had no problem filling it with our countless wedding gifts, souvenirs, and trinkets. We had glasses of all different shapes, sizes, and intended uses, and these took up one whole section of the cabinet.

The fact that I had made use of every inch of the display cabinet did not stop me from purchasing more items to collect dust. I was earning a decent salary as a head teacher, and thus even after paying both my daughters' school fees, I was still left with some money to play around with. My monthly treat was to buy myself a Swarovski crystal ornament, usually a flower, bird, or other animal. I had always liked sparkly things, or "bling", as Tandy called them. These expensive decorations eventually needed their own glass cabinet so that they could be admired from all angles. Fossils and rocks housing stunning gems also had designated space in the cabinet on the shelves below the Swarovski sparklers. I loved my treasures in this transparent chest. Everyone who visited had to view them, and visitors were always suitably impressed.

Imagine my horror, then, when out of the blue, one of the shelves in the Swarovski cabinet plummeted onto the shelf below, smashing the treasures there! Maybe it was caused by the weight of the excessive number of ornaments on that shelf, or maybe it had not been correctly installed in the first place—who knows? What I do know is that a great deal of damage was done. I was in tears. Once I had recovered from the shock of the disaster, I managed to rescue those pieces which were not so badly affected. I was able to stick some back together with superglue but left others to be permanently disfigured. The latter were pushed to the back of the shelf so that they could not be scrutinised too closely. This was the first indication from the Universe that my obsession with luxurious and unnecessary items was not in line with my spiritual needs.

This was not the only minor calamity that transpired during our habitation of our dream house. We nearly lost the whole house before we even finished it! The house had a slate-tile floor throughout to make it appear more spacious and give a unified effect. Although we had wanted a natural appearance, the slate required a lacquer coating to protect it from wear and tear. Shepherd, our domestic worker, and William, a casual worker, were tasked with the job of coating the entire floor one Saturday morning. The double patio doors were left wide open during the operation to speed up the drying process and disperse the strong chemical smell.

While sorting out my bedroom cupboards, I was disturbed by a sudden shout from the main part of the house. I thought one of the dogs had run into the house and knocked the pot of lacquer over, so I was not prepared for what I saw when I put my head around the panel that hid the entrance to the main bedroom. Flames were shooting upwards towards the ceiling in the area where the dining room and kitchen met. At first, I could not fathom where the burning demons had originated from. The whole section was on fire! By some stroke of luck, Shepherd and William had been watering plants earlier and had left one ten-litre bucket of water on the stoep. They quickly used this blessing to quell the main source of the flames, which turned out to be the container of lacquer. But the fire had not started in that container.

In the early days, we were not yet connected to electricity, so to keep at least some food cold, we had a small paraffin fridge running. At the bottom of the fridge was a tiny pilot light, which kept the paraffin burning. While applying the lacquer in the kitchen area, William had gotten close to the fridge, unaware of the danger lurking within. In just a few seconds, the flammable liquid had been ignited, and the fire had raced across the lacquered slate floor towards the source of that liquid, burning furiously as it went.

My heart leapt out of my chest and into my mouth. I was unable to speak as I watched the drama unfold. The flames were doused with water and fortunately disappeared as quickly as they had arrived. Extensive burn and smoke damage had been done to the pine panelling on the walls and ceiling in the kitchen area, but it could have been so much worse. The boys had started their task from the kitchen heading towards the sitting room. If they had started from the other end, coating the entire floor before getting to the fridge, the fire would have spread over a much larger area and resulted in much greater damage. That was a narrow escape, I thought, breathing a huge sigh of relief. Little did I know that I would be face to face with the unforgiving flames just a few years later.

While the construction of the dream house and dream school and the acquisition of possessions appeared to represent great progress in my life, I could not ignore the need to work on my inner self. Reducing my anxiety and stress levels had long ago moved from being optional to being essential due to the shadow caused by my heart condition. Although I already recognised that I needed to understand the importance of living in peace and develop a positive attitude for the sake of my physical well-being, I was also becoming increasingly aware of a need to find some sort of spiritual direction. *The Journey*, written by Brandon Bays, was one of the first books that helped me on my journey. The idea that trauma impacts the body, leaving its imprint in cell memory, made perfect sense to me, so much so that I attended Journey workshops and met with trained practitioners. That enabled me to do a lot of inner work. These sessions gave me insight into the power of forgiveness.

The connection between our mental and emotional states and our physical conditions was made much clearer to me by Louise Hay in *How to Heal Your Life*. She pointed out direct links between bodily symptoms and the specific unhealthy thoughts that caused them. Furthermore, she identified the healthy positive affirmations that would dissolve those causes and thus heal the body. *The Secret* was another major influence for me when it arrived on the self-help scene. I was blown away by what the spiritual gurus in the movie had to say about the law of attraction. They all basically reported the same basic principle: what you ask from the Universe you will receive. The great thing was that one did not have to do anything to get such rewards apart from believing that they were already on their way. (I now know that there is another important step required for this to happen—action!) I learned that positive thoughts not only made you feel good but could actually manifest great stuff into your life. More pertinent for me was the concept that life did not just happen to you; you are not a pawn in the chess game of life but rather the player moving the pieces. Rhonda Byrne's second book, *The Power*, continued along the same lines. The premise that like attracts like made perfect sense to me. No one is cursed or plagued by bad luck unless they think they are! I particularly liked the idea that not only could you find something positive in all situations but it was necessary to do so if you wanted more of the good stuff and less of the bad.

Chapter 6

At the start of 2010, all was going pretty well in my life. I was fifty-two years old, my heart condition was under control, and I had two beautiful and intelligent daughters, a sweet and helpful stepson, a stable and happy marriage, and a stunning, ornament-filled house, which people loved to visit. (They loved to visit us too!)

Careerwise, I had returned to Gaborone Private High School after thirteen years away. I had bailed out from Greenfields English Medium Primary after less than a year when I was offered an exciting position in Gaborone. At first, I had enjoyed the challenge of being the first head teacher in a brand-new school with the responsibility of putting in all the systems from scratch and choosing my own staff at Kgale Hill English Medium Primary School, but I had been met with limitations from the management that I found unacceptable. The school had so much potential, and we were on our way to achieving great things, especially in sport. But over time, I deduced that the management and I didn't have the same vision for the school. Fortunately, once again, as one door closed, another opened. I was offered the position of deputy vice principal at Gaborone Private High School on an even better salary than my current one. More importantly, I found myself working with many old friends and acquaintances, including the new principal, Mr Ramdan. And the icing on the cake was that I was returning to teach in the art department that I had initiated all those years ago!

The head of the art department was Rose Kailash, and from the first time I met this amazing lady, our souls connected. For a start, we were both named after flowers. I had a short meeting with my ex-colleague who now ran the school, and then I was taken to the art rooms and introduced to Rose. We were left alone to talk about what my new role in the department would entail. However, the conversation very quickly transformed into a discussion of our spiritual beliefs. Three times during our talk, my knees literally gave way, and I had to collect myself both physically and emotionally. We both believed in the law of attraction and the power of being present, and Rose was a Journey practitioner too! She asked me to wait while she dived into the storeroom/office, which separated to the two art rooms. Rose re-emerged clutching a small box in her hand. "This is for you, Lily," she said as she handed over the special gift. It was a box of affirmation cards written by Louise Hay. Rose could not have given me a more appropriate or useful present, and yet we had only just met. I think we both knew at the time that we had each found our soulmate.

My return to Gaborone Private High School was just like coming home. It was very comforting to be working in a familiar environment with lots of familiar faces despite being in a completely different role. I even had a girl in one of my classes who was the daughter of a student I had taught during my first round at Gaborone High School. Luckily, she was not as naughty as her father had been.

In addition to the roles of assistant to the vice principal and art teacher, I was introduced to the teaching some subjects that were completely foreign to me as an instructor—English language and literature. Regardless of the fact that I was only given classes in forms one and two, I was quite relieved when I was able to drop the latter subject. Teaching the English language, on the other hand, meant I had to be constantly thumbing through the pages of the *Oxford Advanced Learner's Dictionary* and to relearn basic sentence structure and grammar, which turned out to be great preparation for writing this book. I also found myself leading group discussions on various guidance and counselling topics, which would have been interesting if it not for the general apathy towards this subject shown by most of the students that I encountered.

At this point, I had a thriving vegetable garden situated conveniently next to the kitchen door of our beautiful house. Originally, we had just dug beds into the heavy clay soil and planted a variety of everyday vegetables and herbs. One of the herbs was mint. With the good summer rainfall and regular watering from the borehole, the mint was very happy. In fact, it was so happy that it started spreading at an alarming rate, appearing in beds that had been earmarked for other plants and then quickly taking over as the new inhabitant. The mint's intrusive roots burrowed under the beds, and the vivacious herb ultimately monopolised the whole vegetable garden. This left us with no choice but to dig up the entire planting area in an attempt to remove the offending mint roots.

Metre upon metre of unbreakable root was removed from the garden, but it was impossible to get rid of it all. Now the challenge was how to stop the mint from regenerating and taking over again. The solution was to lay agricultural plastic before constructing brick raised beds. I must admit, it was fun designing the shapes of the brick beds to fit in the area and to make an artistic maze of pathways. However, I discovered later on that there was a fundamental design flaw in my plan: I had not made the paths wide enough for a wheelbarrow to pass through, resulting everything having to be carried in buckets when filling the beds. Eventually, they did get filled with a good mix of clay soil, sandy soil, lots of compost, and organic fertiliser. This became the formula for dealing with our clay soil on a much bigger scale in the future.

Vegetables and herbs planted in these new raised beds grew extremely well, so much so that I ended up with more than we as a family could eat or give away to neighbours and friends. Fortunately, markets had started to appear on the Gaborone scene by that time, providing local entrepreneurs with an interface where they could sell to the public. So, I decided to join them to avoid wasting my lovely produce and make a few thebes in the process.

Meeting people who were concerned for their health and that of the environment further fuelled my commitment to growing as close to 100 per cent organic as I could. Through the markets, I made many new friends—like-minded people who visited my stall. On top of that, there was a great camaraderie between the stall holders; we encouraged each other and bought products internally. In some instances, if it hadn't been for the sales I made to other stall holders, it would hardly have been worth attending the market. In any case, it was not all about the sales on the day. The connections I made ensured that my business would continue to grow and prosper. Within a short space of time, I learnt the importance of marketing and got business cards, price lists, and flyers printed to distribute to interested parties.

The markets were run by different individuals, mainly those who were stall holders themselves and who had access to suitable venues for holding markets. One of the early markets, which lasted well over a year, was held inside a school. Another took place at two-month intervals inside Crafts Botswana, which housed a shop, a restaurant, and a paved entertainment area, while still another was held periodically in the car park of the Craft Centre, a group of shops selling unique and locally produced items—two completely different venues both of which added to the ambiance of those markets. There was a lot of organisation involved in a regular market, and this was usually done in addition to the organiser's day job. Thus, it is not so surprising that these markets had limited shelf lives.

On Saturday, 6 March 2010, I was taking part in one of the markets at a new venue, a restaurant in Mokolodi Village, which was just outside Gaborone. Three days earlier I had celebrated my dear mum's birthday for the first time without her being physically present on the planet. She had died on 16 October the previous year, and thus her loss was still very fresh and sore. After suffering a major stroke in 2004, my sweet and humble mother could not survive without twenty-four-hour care. My brother had located a warm and friendly nursing home near to where he lived, and we moved her there. The nursing staff took great care of our mum, but despite this, her health gradually deteriorated over the years. At the age of 81, confined to her bed, she decided that she had had enough and gently slipped away into the spirit world to join those she loved who had left before her.

I was feeling rather low when the day started, but participating in a market always recharged my batteries. Sharing my stall with an energetic young man, John Green, who was selling his wonderful flower-scented natural honey also made me feel better. On my side of the table was a range of leafy vegetables and herbs, plus a few of the preserves I had started to produce. My younger daughter, Tandy, was there to assist in setting up the stall and selling to the public, and that made participation in the market even more enjoyable.

All was going so well until John, returning from a trip around the stalls, said gravely, "Lily your house is on fire, and I am not kidding. It sounds really bad!" It was difficult to comprehend the words at first. It took time for them to sink in and for the shock to pass to allow me to get back to reality. John took control of the situation and stated that he would pack up my stuff. He instructed me to drive home immediately with Tandy. I look around. Where was Tandy? Someone said that they'd seen my daughter heading for the toilets. I found her shut in one of the cubicles crying, even though we didn't know at that point the true extent of the disaster that lay ahead of us. I coaxed her out and into the Pajero with me. I drove down the winding village road at speed until we reached the main road. Already, we could see the wisps of black smoke in the distant sky. There was no doubt about it— this was a serious fire.

It was a long and terrible journey home. Keeping some kind of positivity going was so difficult when every kilometre closer to our destination just made the smoke more apparent, more real. I needed to keep strong for both Tandy's emotional state and my own, and I needed to drive safely, as we already had one disaster to face. Somewhere along the way, two fire engines caught up with us. We were racing to the same place. Driving through Ruretse, neither Tandy nor I could speak. I felt nauseous with the fear of what we were about to witness. As we approached our bright-green gates, we still couldn't view the house, but the billowing black smoke told its own story.

I drove halfway down the drive and came to an abrupt halt. Neighbours were standing motionless at the edge of the garden, and I jumped out of the car and joined them. I don't think I even switched the engine off—that was done later. Our beautiful house was a mass of orange flames and thick black smoke. It was too much to take in. I dropped to the ground. Time seemed to stand still, and I just lay there in another world. I don't remember getting up, but

I somehow found myself being led to the ambulance that had been following the fire engines. Unfortunately, apart from a stretcher bed, there weren't any medical apparatuses in the ambulance, so I really don't know to this day what the purpose of its presence at the scene was. Cheryl, who had supported me on my way to the ambulance, took over as the nurse and gave me some drops of Rescue Remedy and then got me to lie down on the stretcher. "Where is Tandy?" I asked her as I came back to my senses. Cheryl immediately rushed off to look for my 18-year-old daughter. She found Tandy wandering aimlessly down the gravel road. It was all too much for her too. Cheryl gently led her back and brought her to the ambulance to sit with me while I started to take stock of the situation. Stuart was deep in Lobatse doing water divining. As soon as he got the news, he headed back home, but it took him nearly two hours to make that same painful journey. By then, I had pulled myself together and gathered up the courage to get closer to the raging inferno. I started to piece together the information from Shepherd, the guys who had been doing maintenance work on the front stoop, and those first to arrive on the scene of the drama.

The painters had seen smoke coming towards them from the back of the house. They had reported this to Shepherd, who'd then left the scullery where he had been washing dishes to investigate. He'd walked up and down the house, but there had been no sign of anything amiss in the open-plan main room. Just as Shepherd had opened Tandy's bedroom door, the two gas cylinders next to the scullery had exploded. Hot flames had lashed through the open bedroom door, and Shepherd had had to make a hasty retreat out of the house. It had been a very lucky escape for young Shepherd but not for the wooden house. By then, the fire had been burning furiously at both ends, and in no time, the whole building had begun to collapse. Shepherd and the painters had tried their best to pull out my brand-new, state-of-the-art stove before the roof came down, but it had been just too heavy and they'd only had minutes before the inevitable happened. Finally, the metal roof had come crashing down, creating a huge, enclosed furnace where the fire could rage unabated. People in the Ruretse community who had arrived on the scene had picked up hose pipes and turned on the taps, but nothing had happened. One of the first casualties of the fire had been the power, and no electricity meant no water from the borehole. We arrived soon after.

The fire engines that arrived with me attempted to save the day by showering the burning mass with water from all sides. The fire slowed down for some minutes and then continued on its course of destruction, incinerating everything enclosed within the fallen roof. Eventually, the fire officers had to admit there was nothing they could do to stop the merciless fire. One blessing was that the other building on the plot, a small wood-panelled cottage, was far enough away to be unaffected by the fire. A young couple were renting it, and the mother was home at that time with two very young children. She heard the commotion but could only watch helplessly with a baby in her arms and a 2-year-old by her side. The lawn in front of this cottage became my refuge and viewing arena as the main house continued to burn to nothing. The distance between them allowed me to be spared the details of the destruction taking place. That did not stop my heart from hurting, however. I may not have been able to witness all my possessions going up in smoke, but I didn't need to, as my imagination filled in the blanks.

When Stuart finally arrived, he stood there in disbelief. More accurately, he didn't *want* to believe his eyes. He was affectionately known as Mr Fix-it, but there was nothing he could do to repair the situation this time. Friends followed shortly afterwards, bringing whatever they could to help lessen the blow—mostly beer and wine. One close friend of mine, Melanie, brought something much healthier: a beautiful dish containing mixed fruits. That colourful, spotted dish is one of my favourite serving dishes to this day. Mel must have been a girl guide when younger, as she also brought us a bag of assorted essential toiletries. I had a quiet chuckle to myself later on that day, as it included a box of Tampax. She had forgotten that I had had a hysterectomy over ten years before.

The evening seemed endless. The fire engines had long retreated, safe in the knowledge that their presence no longer served any purpose. The fire simply had to run its course until it finally devoured every item imprisoned under the roof. Some of Stuart's buddies started a braai on the lawn. At least the fire they made was under control. Although we spent very little time together as a couple, everyone who joined us during that night gave us love and support. But all their kind words could not sugar-coat the fact that we had lost nearly all our worldly possessions in just a few smouldering hours.

Normally, you wake up from a nightmare, but that Sunday morning, waking up brought us back to the nightmare. The only thing left of our beautiful home was a crumpled metal roof with smoke still seeping out if it. And if that weren't bad enough, the realisation that we had no power and thus no water set off some new alarm bells. We could easily ship in enough water for our personal needs, but what about all the trees and plants in our huge garden? Admittedly, several trees near the house had already been reduced to charcoal, but there were still plenty worth saving.

Out of this situation emerged a hero in the form of Philip McGregor, my ex-student and, later on, my good friend. He worked with electrical installations, and after several hours, he managed to temporarily get power and water back. This was not his only heroic act as far as my heart was concerned. Throughout the morning, I was unable to get closer to the disaster site. I sat on the lawn in front of the cottage in a daze, not wanting to come face to face with reality. Yes, I could see the outline of the devastating scene through the iron gates to our house and garden, but I could not find the courage to walk through them. It was as if they were a barrier separating me from the nightmare, and yet they no longer served any real purpose. But Philip took me by the hand and gently whispered, "Let's go." As we ventured through the gates of hell, he put his arm around me, reassuring me that I could cope with the spectre beyond.

It was now late morning, and the remaining ashes had cooled down, enabling two wonderful friends to pick up a few remnants of our possessions. However, I am not exaggerating when I say that the fire had created a disappearing act of mammoth proportions. In most cases, after a house fire, there is some indication that furniture and appliances had once existed. Not this time! Televisions, refrigerators, my state-of-the-art stove, numerous cupboards, huge tables, and our wall-length display cabinet had seemingly dissolved into thin air. A few bed springs remained to indicate that there had once been bedrooms, but there was not much else. Later on, some survivors were found in the debris; a pottery set from Thamaga and my own clay artwork that I'd produced at college many years ago were found, surprisingly, in perfect condition. The pottery items had been fired at an equally high temperature and thus had not been affected by the intense heat of the inferno from the previous day. There was also plenty of broken ceramic-ware scattered throughout what had been the kitchen and dining room. Whole dinner and tea sets were indirect casualties of the fire. As burning cupboards and shelves had collapsed, the contents had dropped to the floor and simply smashed into pieces.

Glass and metal ornaments, including prized silver trophies and inherited treasures, had melted into unrecognisable forms. And this time, my Swarovski crystal collection was completely destroyed, never to be resurrected again. My own treasured artworks were gone. I regretted having brought my large, three-dimensional textile picture home after thinking it had spent too long in my office at school. It had taken three weeks to sew and embroider the delicate spray of orchids, and I had been very proud of the finished product. Also gone was a beautiful pencil portrait of Tandy in which Bella had painstakingly and accurately captured the likeness of her sister. Such masterpieces are irreplaceable.

Countless wedding gifts of various materials, which had had the sole purpose of taking up space and collecting dust, were now dust themselves. The wardrobes filled with my excessive collection of clothing for every season were as invisible as their contents. Computers and laptops were gone along with all their data. The five chapters of the book I'd been writing about the loves in my mother's life were now just a hidden memory file in the computer in my head.

All the research work, poems, and paintings dedicated to my dear mother, Sylvia, were also reduced to just memories.

Stuart and Tandy had lost all their personal possessions too. Bella had been more fortunate, as most of her belongings were in the flat she inhabited near Pretoria University. Darren had long moved out with all his clothes and electronic gadgets, so he was also a lucky one. Not so lucky were the people who had kindly lent us CDs, DVDs, or anything else, as they were now on permanent loan.

Our four cats and four dogs reappeared on the scene one by one once they felt it was safe to do so. They had been emotionally affected but had suffered no physical damage. The fish in the aquarium in the sitting room were not so blessed. They'd had no means to escape their glass prison, and by the time it had broken open, they had probably already been cooked.

The only consolation from the complete incineration of almost all our possessions was that there was no chance of fixing anything. It was just a matter of throwing all the scraps into a big skip to be taken away. The two determined ladies, Carol Wick and Judith Porter, who had spent hours skimming through the wreckage had managed to find some gems that could be recycled. One of them, Carol, later made them into colourful wind chimes and decorated pavers. The jigsaw pieces of the main dinner set were collected into a box, where they remained until finally joining the rest of our belongings at the local landfill.

Chapter 7

To be honest, the days that followed our home burning down are a bit of a blur. A sort of numbness set in, as if I had been hypnotised to shield my mind and soul from the pain of the loss. In retrospect, I realise that I had to go through all the stages one associates with the loss of a loved one. It was a long grieving process which needed time, love, and support to aid the healing. Stuart and I went through this separately. His initial coping tactic was distracting himself by drinking beer with his mates—it almost seemed like there was a party going on that day of the fire with that braai! Then he moved into his usual valuable mode of assessing what action was needed and focusing fully on getting it done. I don't think he considered that he needed to heal from this great loss; he just shoved it down into some deep recess in his soul.

As for me, healing was of utmost importance. I was on a mission to find something positive out of this life-changing experience so that I could let it go and move forward. The person who was fundamental to my recovery was my eldest daughter, my beloved Bella. She returned the day after the fire from Pretoria, where she was studying aeronautical engineering. I knew that I needed her more than anyone else, and I awaited her arrival with a conviction that she would make everything all right. And that is exactly what she did.

Just catching a glimpse of Bella as she hurriedly got out of the car already sent waves of relief through my body. She immediately put her arm around me, something Stuart had yet to do, and guided me quietly away from all the well-wishers and helpers lodging on the lawn. "It will be all right," Bella assured me, and I knew it was true. She led me to the meditation area, a secluded part of the "jungle garden", which at that time was shaded by indigenous trees. The huge mound of rocks where the lapa had been built was on the left behind us. We sat on the wooden bench, Bella's arm still around my shoulders holding me close to her heart. In a voice of experience and authority, she asked, "Mum, what was in the kitchen?" I slowly started to list the equipment and fittings, beginning with my state-of-the-art stove, of course. Whenever I hesitated, she gently nudged me to continue until all the memorable items had been named. Then Bella commanded me to say goodbye to them, and as I obediently surrendered to the instruction, they disappeared from my short-term memory forever.

I don't know how long it took, but we continued with this process until all the rooms had been exorcised of their material contents. How did a twenty-one-year-old student know what I needed on my journey of healing from the damage done by the fire? Maybe Bella was more than she appeared to be in her physical form. What I do know is that the healing from the loss of the house and everything in it had begun.

The same friend who had rescued me and Tandy on that terrible day did us a further act of kindness, which also contributed to me finding a way forward. Some days later, Cheryl Grant brought a gift of hope—twenty packets of vegetable and herb seeds to enable me to restart my kitchen garden. The food garden had been strategically positioned so that I merely had to step out of the kitchen side door to arrive in my own vegetable store. Of course, with it so close to the burning house, all but a few plants had been destroyed. The lemon grass had shielded the herbs behind it, but that was all that remained. Replanting the vegetable garden was an integral part of my healing. It brought with it an awareness that I could start again and once more enjoy the fruits of my labour.

Our house and possessions had not yet been insured, although I'd been in the process of getting it done. As a result, the financial loss had hurtled us back to the position of a young couple starting out in life. However, not only were we fortunate enough to still have our vehicles intact, but we also had a four-acre plot. It took time before we could start counting our blessings, but the plot was indeed a great one.

Friends and ex-colleagues knowing our financial position got together and organised a fundraising event for us. The "family fun day" was to take place at the cricket club one April Sunday, a few weeks after the fire. Not only would it be an opportunity for money to be raised on our behalf, but it would be the first time since the fire that we would have the chance to interact with many good friends in a more relaxed and happy setting. However, I underestimated the emotional effects that the reunion would have on me.

On the morning of the event, Stuart went on ahead to help with the set-up, and I remained behind to finish chores at home and then prepare myself. I had woken up feeling nauseous (three glasses of whisky the night before hadn't helped), and before long, I started being violently sick. It was so intense that I passed out and found myself on the floor, totally disoriented. I tried to call Stuart but couldn't get through to him, and I was soon back on the cold slate tiles. Instinctively, I called Cheryl, who took me to her house so she could monitor what was going on with me.

I lay on the bed in the Grants' spare bedroom with a large glass of water by my side. When I awoke from the next attack, I was lying in a pool of water and broken glass. I managed to find Cheryl and apologised for the breakage, and she took away the damage. I returned to lying on the bed, but it was only a few minutes before the next exhausting episode occurred. By this time, Cheryl and Adam had assessed that I needed urgent medical help, as there were no signs of this saga coming to an end. They called MedRescue and arranged to meet the ambulance en route, since Ruretse is well out of town.

Adam drove at high speed while I sat next to him in the front passenger's seat of the four-by-four truck. We had not gotten very far down the gravel road when we had to come to a grinding halt so that I could try to vomit again. The next thing I knew, I was hanging out of the truck with only the seat belt stopping my fall. I collected myself back into the vehicle, but I was now in fear of a repeat performance. I tried my best to avoid it, but the nausea continued unabated. Ironically, we met the ambulance not far from the cricket club where the fundraising event was now in full swing. Adam had aimed to catch up with Stuart there so that he could take over his wife's care, but the ambulance intervened and rushed me straight to hospital.

During the journey to the hospital, I was given medication to stop the nausea, but it failed to stop the attacks, which continued even in the emergency room. I was then put on a drip with more medication, and eventually the drama came to an end. Shortly afterwards, Stuart and Adam arrived along with a few concerned friends, and I started feeling better. Once again, I had witnessed how powerfully emotions controlled my body. Needless to say, I missed the entire event, and friends who had gathered were disappointed not to meet up with me.

The money raised from the fun day was added to individual donations both from close friends and, amazingly, from people we hardly knew! The huge amount of P10,000 was generously handed over to us by a building company. The directors of that company knew us from a distance and had heard about our tragedy. They explained that they simply wanted to help us rebuild our lives. The total we received was over P40,000, but that was far from enough to even start thinking of building another house. Our good friend Edwin had built a small cottage on our plot to stay in over the weekends, but he was no longer using it. The money we were given was sufficient to revamp Edwin's cottage, which we had already moved into, and construct our first vegetable "tunnel".

The young people who had been renting the cottage were offered free accommodation in Gaborone, which was much more convenient for them, as the husband worked in the city. Again, Judith had come to our rescue. We had plenty of offers for free accommodation too, including from my ex-boss at Montle Primary School. Most of them would have been useful as a temporary solution but not for taking care of our animals. We decided that moving into the little cottage would solve the problem and enable us to start picking up the pieces of our lives, both figuratively and literally.

As well as making some improvements to the one-bedroom cottage, we needed somewhere for our children to sleep when they visited. Stuart came up with the idea of putting up two wooden cabins with a space in between and covering them with one single corrugated-iron roof sheet to help keep them cool. The centre section would later be turned into his workshop. One of the cabins was to be used as our TV room but could double as a bedroom if more than one child arrived on the scene, while the other became both Tandy's bedroom and the ironing room.

Stuart and I didn't have to worry about furniture and kitchen equipment. We were showered with sofas, beds, a dining room suite, and chairs, not to mention an abundance of refrigerators and freezers! In fact, we ended up with more of these items than we had space for, so the extras were stored in a container at the servant's quarters. Several of the refrigerators did not work too well and eventually ended up as storage containers on the farm. Clothing, shoes, kitchenware, tableware, and so on, were also given to us in overflowing quantities. Again, some of the donors were very well known to us, but others were complete strangers touched by our story. If there is ever a time that a community comes together as one, it is when a major tragedy hits people close to home. And that is a time to truly value the compassion of those around you, as without them, you could quietly slip down into a deep hole of depression.

As 2010 progressed, the seeds of hope began to germinate. Stuart and I were both soon able to return to our respective jobs and the routines of daily life that accompanied them. Bella went back to the University of Pretoria, also known as Tuks, in South Africa, where she continued to excel despite the odds being stacked against her. Most of the handful of girls studying aeronautical engineering dropped out as the course went on, and quite a few of the boys did too. The course was very demanding of any student even without additional challenges, let alone for a girl whose family had just lost their home and all their worldly possessions and were now having to start from scratch. Bella showed herself to be made of sterner stuff with a drive and tenacity that left her friends and family in awe. She was approaching the last year of the degree with a crucial final project to undertake, but instead of slowing down, she accelerated like an athlete in their final lap!

My other daughter had fortunately completed her secondary education and was on a gap year when the house burned down. Plans had already been finalised for Tandy to go to Holland to work as an au pair looking after two small children. It was expected to be a good experience where she could learn about another country and earn some pocket money too. About a month after losing the house, we took her to the airport, but already I could see uneasiness had crept in. After only a few days with the lovely family who had welcomed Tandy into their lives, she wanted to come home. Although I managed to persuade her to stay, she told the empathetic parents that she felt like she was losing her home for the second time and was desperate to return to it. Once this was relayed to my ears, I knew that we had to make plans for her to leave Holland.

I suggested to Tandy that instead of coming straight back to Botswana, she should stay with my brother and his family in the United Kingdom for a few weeks. After all, I had already paid for the return flight from Holland, and with just a little more money, her journey could be diverted to add a stop in London before flying to Botswana. There was no rush for Tandy to come home and getting to know her four cousins would help to take her mind off recent events. Meanwhile, Stuart and I could work on transforming the cottage and cabins into a more comfortable place for her to stay when she got back.

Despite our new accommodation being a quarter of the size of our previous one, it was surprisingly more than satisfactory. Most of what we now possessed were functional items. There was no space for anything that did not perform a practical task. I slowly began to realise that I did not need a huge mansion filled with objects requiring regular cleaning and repositioning to be happy. On the contrary, my life had become simpler and less stressful. I was experiencing a new kind of freedom where I could spend less time focusing on the world of form and more on the world of spirit. This realisation was part of my healing from an experience that was equivalent to any other loss and thus required a period of grieving and self-love. I don't think Stuart went through the same process, and for years after, he remained determined to build a replacement mansion and seemed to make his happiness dependent on that goal.

Part Three

The Development of Resilience: Difficult Growing Conditions Result in a Stronger Plant

Do not judge me by my successes, judge me by how many times I fell down and got back up again.

—Nelson Mandela

Strength and resilience are like muscles; they need to be exercised in order for them to increase. Challenging experiences, like those I had already gone through up to this point in my story, were certainly a good workout. Plants which have been grown in perfect conditions with regular watering usually don't do too well when those conditions change. The recent seven-year drought in Botswana has seen many exotic plants fall by the wayside, as they could not handle the high temperatures and lack of water, while indigenous varieties, growing in poor soil with little water, were hardly affected. That's why it is advisable to stop watering certain plants for short intervals to make their roots look for water deep in the soil, resulting in a stronger root system. This gives the plants a greater ability to survive and even thrive when conditions get even tougher. They become resilient.

Chapter 8

At the time of our house burning down, I was back working at Gaborone High School, the first private school I had taught at thirteen years before. I had been there barely three months when the disaster hit, but I was with old colleagues and friends who rallied round to give me support at several different levels. The management of the school donated P5,000, and the staff had no problem in matching that amount, doubling the donation. My head of department and soulmate, Rose, was my constant companion, both in and out of school, and several other teachers offered psychological and material support.

One teacher's kindness, I will never forget, helped me survive winter when it arrived. Amongst the clothing donations we'd received, there was not one outer garment, and it had started getting very cold. One chilly day in June, Lesego, who taught mathematics at Gaborone High School, declared that she had too many winter jackets and was happy to give one of them away. The next day, she brought to school not a plain overcoat but a beautiful, mock-sheepskin-lined, heavyweight coat and announced that it was now mine.

During the week, working with wonderful colleagues like Lesego and teaching enthusiastic students was a great distraction from the disaster of losing all our possessions. Meanwhile, at the weekends, my first vegetable tunnel was being constructed from gum poles, wire, old tyres, and shade netting, and that gave us hope of a better future. To hold the poles upright and support the shade netting, deep holes were dug on either side of the tunnel, and the tyres with wire attached were dropped inside. The holes were then refilled with our heavy clay soil. There was no need to use cement, as the clay, when dry, was not going anywhere. The wire was nailed to the top of the gum poles, and the shade netting strips were sewn together before being placed over the wire, secured at intervals with nails.

Given that the soil on our plot was mostly clay, I had already seen the advantage of using raised beds with my original vegetable garden. We did not have enough funds to build brick beds all down the forty-metre vegetable tunnel, so an alternative needed to be found. This is where the only remaining part of the house came into good use. We used the burnt corrugated iron sheets from the roof to build the sides of the raised beds. They did not fill the whole tunnel, but at least these beds covered two-thirds of the area. This was just the start of the recycling that was to become an integral part of the farm's character and form.

Fortunately, we had a large compost heap prepared to provide nutrients and improve the soil texture of the large garden. Its contents were simply diverted to the raised beds along with a mixture of clay, river sand, agricultural lime, dried chicken manure, and bonemeal. It proved to be a winning combination, as a single packet of mixed lettuce seeds gave us enough plants to fill nearly all the raised beds in the tunnel. I sowed the seeds in one of the beds, and every single seed must have germinated. Shepherd and I transplanted the robust lettuce seedlings over the course of several days until the mission was completed.

At the time we planted the lettuce seedlings during the spring of 2010, the weather was farmer friendly, with a gentle rise in temperature followed by summer rainfall. The lettuce thrived and appeared to have immunity to any kind of disease or pest infestation. Not only did we have enough lettuce for the upcoming markets; we had lettuce for Africa! Stuart's close friend Edwin asked the management of the Eagle's Nest, a pub and restaurant in the centre of Gaborone, if they would be interested in getting heads of lettuce from us. They were very happy with the sample that they were presented with, and for many years thereafter I continued to supply them with mixed lettuce and Swiss chard (which some people call spinach).

The principal of Gaborone High School, Mr Ramdan, came to the plot shortly after the house burnt down. He and his teacher wife witnessed first-hand the destruction and the tough situation I found myself in. Later that year, when I needed to get my produce to the Eagle's Nest, I had to ask Mr Ramdan for a big favour. I knew I couldn't leave the school during the morning classes, so the solution I devised was for the driver from the restaurant to collect the order from my vehicle in the school car park during tea break. Mr Ramadan agreed to this system of delivery, which would go on to work well for several years. A few months later, I was able to sell a variety of vegetables to my colleagues and the office staff too. All the income from these sales and those made at the monthly markets went into further developing what was now becoming a fast-growing farm.

The second tunnel to be built was very similar to the first, but we had used up all the burnt roofing. We had already learnt that raised beds were much easier to prepare and use than beds made by digging trenches in the unforgiving clay. Cheryl came to our rescue for the third time. She and Adam had bought a house in Ruretse with an existing prefab wall. The wall was not what they wanted, and they promptly had it dismantled and delivered to our plot The slabs of concrete were ideal as sides of the raised beds. We just needed to close the ends with a few bricks and cement. The large number of slabs created enough beds to fill the entire length of one side of the tunnel. Now we just had the space on the left-hand side of that tunnel to utilise.

Stuart and his buddy got to work on nailing wooden boards together to make an inner and outer frame. They then poured concrete mix between the two and left it to set. This turned out to be not only a slow process but also an expensive one, and so only eight of these state-of-the-art beds were completed. However, they were deeper than the other raised beds, so they became the home for root vegetables, which welcomed the additional depth. The remaining section of the tunnel, except for a vacant area right at the back, was made into trench beds. Some months later, Stuart had the brilliant idea of cutting slices from a damaged water tank and converting them into oval raised beds to fit in that space. Tunnel two was now complete.

In October 2011, I decided to turn my rapidly expanding hobby into a formal business. After all, I was already supplying the Eagle's Nest with lettuce and Swiss chard on a regular basis—three times a week, to be exact. Coming up with a business name took some thought. I was using organic practices in the farm and did not use any chemicals, but I had not been certified, so I could not use the word *organic* for my company. The nearest I could get to stating that I supply organically grown vegetables and herbs was to say that my farm was working with nature. Hence, the company was registered as Nature's Friend.

This was my first experience at running my own business, but at least I had enrolled with MANCOSA in 2004 to do a certificate in business management. The idea behind studying this course had been to prepare myself for managing Greenfields School in Moshupa, which would require skills in addition to those required for heading a school. I had particularly needed to learn about financial administration and human resource management. It had only been a one-year course, but as usual, I had fully engaged in doing the best I could in each module, even though the outcome would simply be pass or fail. Now, the coursebooks for the modules served as useful sources of information while I was setting up my own business.

On the family front, Thandiwe had now started university. Originally, she had been interested in studying architecture at Pretoria University, where Bella was about to start her final year. However, due to a number of reasons, she ended up enrolling in civil engineering, which could still provide a good grounding for studying architecture at a later date. Tandy, being very different from her sister, did not want to go into one of the university's boarding houses, so we instead found her accommodation in an old but quaint house that had been turned into a commune. The commune offered several advantages. Apart from the building being a homely environment, there were students staying at the commune who were doing the same course as Tandy, and they were only too happy to offer her guidance and support.

Darren was now on course to doing what all my children had vowed not to do, and that was to become a teacher like their mother. The girls were adamant that they would not follow in their mother's footsteps at any cost. My stepson found himself treading the same path as me not by any deliberate action but as a result of following his passion of playing rugby and thus being involved with sport. Darren applied to several schools for a position in their sports departments and was delighted when he was accepted at the same school that his half-brother Eddie was attending. The school specialised in teaching children with learning difficulties, and physical education was recognised as having a fundamental part to play in their all-round development.

At this time, Darren was still living with his mother, stepfather, and half-brother in Johannesburg, and his salary helped him contribute towards his keep. Stuart and I would go to South Africa quite regularly and usually combined our visits, seeing the girls in Pretoria and Darren in Johannesburg. Stuart was working for Crafty Creations, the company that had built our dream house. Although this company always had several projects on the go, Stuart was still able to find the time to help me build up the farm and take a Saturday off here and there for trips to South Africa to buy materials and visit our children and our buddies, the Thompson family.

Bella had moved out of "res" and was now living in a flat on her own near the university. She had split up with her long-term boyfriend Victor. He had left the course that they were both studying and returned to Botswana, and although Bella and Victor had tried to continue their relationship across the miles, it had eventually weakened, and the link had broken. It was not long before Bella got involved with someone else. Barely four months later, she met a young man who was not a university student but was close friends with some of her colleagues. Dumisani also shared some common interests with Bella. After leaving school, he had set up his own computer business, which initially did very well. Bella was a whiz at information technology and had a passion for computer programming. They both also loved music and dancing, which was an integral part of socialising with their joint group of friends.

I soon realised that Bella and Dumisani were very happy together, and thus when Dumisani called me out of the blue to ask for Bella's hand in marriage, it was not a complete surprise. What was more of a surprise was that he was very formal in his request. I didn't think that young people of his generation would speak so eloquently and with so much respect to their girlfriends' mothers. I was particularly impressed when Dumisani spoke of the importance of not rushing the marriage and the need for both sets of parents to meet and become familiar with each other before any arrangements could be made. Furthermore, Dumisani was adamant that any rift in our two families should be healed, and he pinpointed the current situation that existed between Bella and Tandy. The two sisters had had a major falling out the year before and were not even talking to each other. Dumisani was determined that the dispute between them should be resolved so that harmony could be restored in our family. I was very happy that he wanted to be the catalyst for getting my two girls reunited, and thus Dumisani won both my approval of his proposal and my respect for him as a good-hearted young man.

In the months following that life-changing phone call, I got to know Dumisani more intimately, as every time Bella came home to Ruretse, he was by her side. At one of the open farm events in 2011, Dumisani was introduced to a few of my close friends, who found him to be polite and charming. He also spent Christmas and New Year's with us at the end of the same year. Dumisani was fast becoming part of our family. What's more, true to his word, Dumisani managed to get the two sisters back on good terms, and the three of them spent time together having lunch and taking part in other social activities. On top of that, he communicated regularly with me, mostly on Facebook. In fact, Dumisani talked to me more often and more openly than my own daughter!

Bella completed her degree in mechanical engineering in style with 92 per cent score on her final project. It was also recognised as the 'Best Aeronautical Project' by the Aeronautical Society of South

Africa in 2011. She had worked extremely hard, day and night, and fully deserved the distinction she was awarded for her degree. That was not the only award she received either. An aviation company pledged to sponsor Bella to do both her master's and honours in the same subject. The only hitch was that she needed to be a South African citizen—something she had been working on for almost four years already. All sorts of obstacles got in the way of her receiving that document, despite her father reverting to his original South African status. Musa had renounced his Botswanan citizenship some years earlier, having relocated to Mafikeng in South Africa.

Fortunately, the administration at the University of Pretoria were very understanding and allowed Bella to register and start the post-graduate course in February 2012. With her usual determination, she attended lectures and worked on assignments while still trying to get her South African citizenship processed. This involved travelling to both Botswana and Mafikeng to collect the additional papers that were required for her application to be complete.

As time marched on, the situation became very stressful. Although the university had allowed Bella to participate in lectures well into the course, she would not be allowed to sit the fast-approaching examinations without the course fees being paid. The aviation company was not able to release the money without proof that Bella was a South African. At the eleventh hour, I received a simple text message: "I got it!" It was such a relief to know that after all my daughter's efforts, her tenacity had paid off, and she could continue with her master's and write the impending examinations. This joyous news was announced in July 2012, and surely the rest of the year was going to be a breeze in comparison.

My dual life as a teacher and a farmer was keeping me on my toes. Just being an art teacher and the deputy vice principal was pretty demanding in itself, but I was also allocated some English-language and English-literature classes by virtue of being English myself. The latter subject was particularly tough as, if the truth be known, I had little interest in literature, whereas learning about my own language was helping me with my writing skills. I was therefore pleased when

55

I was allowed to drop the English literature class in 2011—that was, until I found out that it was a case of "out of the frying pan and into the fire"! I was given form-four guidance and counselling, which was equally foreign to me as a teaching subject. The fact that the subject was not to be examined left the students disinterested, and it was difficult to motivate them to participate in the lessons.

By contrast, I was enjoying farming immensely. We had completed three tunnels, enabling me to grow a wider of range of vegetables. Trips to South Africa naturally included visits to the extensive nurseries along Bayer's Naude Drive, and there were plenty of plants and seeds to choose from. Some of the racks of seed packets found in Garden World were from Europe, and they included exciting heirloom and organic varieties of vegetables and herbs. Purple cauliflower, red lettuce, pink-and-white-striped beetroots, tomatoes of almost every colour under the sun, and carrots in mixed packets of orange, white, and yellow all found their way into my shopping basket.

To my delight, John Green, my friend and neighbour, came back from America with a catalogue from Baker Creek Heirloom Seed Co. The building which housed its seed bank was literally an old bank. The safe deposit boxes had been converted into handy drawers in which to keep the many seed packets in good order. And if the catalogue was anything to go by, there must have been thousands upon thousands of seeds safely banked. I was like a kid in a candy store rummaging through its pages with my eyes popping out of my head at all the amazing plants I could grow. It took many attempts to whittle down my choice of seeds to the number that I could realistically afford.

Lettuce and Swiss chard were still the main occupants of the tunnels, but I used many of the raised beds to try out weird and wonderful vegetables from South Africa and America. The harvests they produced turned out to be very popular at the markets I regularly took part in. By that time, there was a monthly market at one of the private schools. The school held various events and invited entrepreneurs to hire stalls and hopefully make some good sales. These stalls would benefit the event by attracting more people to attend and adding to the ambience. Thus, not only was I fully occupied during the week with my professional vocation, but at the weekends, I was just as busy with school events, markets, and working on the farm—a full and happy life indeed.

Our trips to South Africa were very much multipurpose. Apart from seeing our children and purchasing plants and seeds (or motorbike parts in Stuart's case), we also enjoyed social activities with our friends the Thompsons in Johannesburg. Elise Thompson and I have a mutual love of gardening, and the beginning of the best growing season was marked by an annual spring festival at Garden World there in the city. This festival was a classical musical show interspersed with interesting talks and giveaways, and it was also an opportunity to visit the show gardens, including South Africa's entry in the Chelsea Garden Show. How they moved it from London to Johannesburg and reconstructed it each year was beyond my comprehension. Unsurprisingly, it was always the main attraction of the show.

For some reason, we missed visiting Johannesburg in 2012 at the time of the festival, so I instead managed to persuade Stuart to attend a fascinating series of demonstrations at Garden World in early September. Just as we were about to enter the auditorium, I received a mysterious call from Dumisani, who by then was my daughter's ex-fiancé. He told me that something had just happened between the two of them but that it was not as bad as Isobel might portray it to be. Well, that of course made me think the opposite, and I quickly tried to call her to get her version of the story. Eventually, I got through to Bella. She sounded a bit disturbed as she explained that they had had an argument over her cell phone. Dumisani had taken it to look at her messages and refused to give it back. Bella had then called the security guard at the entrance to the flats, and as a result, Dumisani had had to return the phone to its owner. Bella assured me that although she was upset with her ex, everything was now settled, so I should not worry. At that point, the talks had started, so we needed to take our seats.

Once the event was over, I called my daughter again and suggested that maybe I could get Darren to collect her from Pretoria so that she could join us at the Thompsons. However, she had already made plans with her sister to go to a spring music festival in Pretoria and gave me further assurance that all was now well.

Back when I'd found out that Bella and Dumisani were no longer dating, the news had come as quite a shock, as my daughter had not told me anything about the break-up. Instead, it had been Dumisani who had sent me a message through Facebook towards the end of July stating that they had decided to call off their engagement for the time being. He had not seemed too concerned about this development in their relationship and had been confident that one day he would still call Isobel his wife. Indeed, the ex-couple had continued to see each other, and Bella had had a short holiday with him in August. Therefore, the split seemed quite amicable, apart from the incident with her phone. Dumisani even allowed Bella to continue living in his flat until the end of the year, when she planned to move in with Tandy. He had organised accommodation for himself with friends in Pretoria North, so it was not a problem for him to move out.

I tried to ask Bella about the breakup, but she always played it down as not being a big deal. I was inclined to believe her, as most times when I called, Dumisani was there in the background. He was clearly still part of Bella's life, indicating that this was a minor hitch in their relationship. Anyway, it would have been awkward to ask her about Dumisani's role in their split with him being present there. So, our conversations were mostly about practical issues, such as renewing Bella's driving licence and when she would next be coming home.

Chapter 9

The pages that follow are not easy for me to write, even though I have gone over the events of the next few days of my life in my mind many times and have also been able to relate the details of this story to a few close friends, eventually without shedding a tear. However, placing the words on paper is much harder. It feels very final, as if once done, I can no longer change what happened. But of course, that is an impossible idea anyway.

When I first started to write this section, I was distracted by some glass bottles being knocked over close to the kitchen door. On closer inspection, I found a large snake making its way around the house to the back garden. When I returned to my writing, something surprised me even more than the snake. A small, fluffy feather was sitting on top of my pen—a sure sign that an angel was with me as I began to empty out my soul.

On Wednesday, 19 September 2012, my dear daughter sent me an email asking me to get a copy of her Botswana driving license certified to enable her to renew it in South Africa. The short message ended with the words that have always meant so much to me: "I love you, Mum." After completing this task and sending the certified copy back to Bella, I decided to check if she had received the email. So, I tried to call her on that Friday morning, but she did not pick up her phone. Stuart also tried to call her and got the same result. When I tried again later in the day, her phone appeared to be off altogether. On Saturday morning, I still could not get through to Bella and was compelled to call Dumisani, but unfortunately, he was also not available.

A few hours later, I was getting rather anxious and tried Dumisani's number again. This time, he answered. My relief was short lived, as Dumisani said that he did not have any idea where Bella was or why she was not answering her phone. Dumisani went on to explain that the last time he'd seen Bella was on Wednesday, when they had had an argument and he had left her alone in the flat. When he'd returned on Thursday, he said, Bella had packed her bag and gone somewhere, though he had no clue as to her destination. He then surprised me by telling me, "You know that guy Steven who is Bella's long-time friend? Well, he is now the new boyfriend!" I replied sharply that I was not interested in the scenario and that all I wanted to know is where to find Bella so that I could talk to her. That was the end to the conversation, as it was clear that he was unable to help me locate my missing daughter.

In the hours that followed that conversation, I found it difficult to get involved in any activities around the house and even on the farm. I didn't want to miss getting the call from Bella and finding out that she was absolutely fine and that, as usual, I had been worrying for nothing. But that call never came. Instead, I received one from Anele Khumalo, who is my ex-sister-in-law and the girls' Aunty. She wanted to know if I was home at the farm so she could come and see me. I should have asked her what the visit was about, but seeing as we were still good friends, she really didn't need a reason.

An hour slipped by, and I was feeling more and more uneasy. I decided to call Anele to find out if she was still on her way to us. The voice at the other end of the line was very emotional. Anele was crying. I asked how far she was from the farm, and Anele replied that she was already at our gate. I obviously sensed something was wrong and wondered if her brother, my ex-husband, had met with an accident.

Anele's car came slowly down the driveway. When it came to a halt, I saw she was not alone. When both her sister and mother got out of the car, I started to shake, and it felt like my heart stopped beating. Stuart went to meet the three tearful women. After a quick exchange of words, he brought them to where I was sitting outside the house. Then he stated clearly and calmly the most terrible words I ever heard: "Bella is dead." Although all the evidence before me told me that he was telling the truth, I spontaneously replied in a defiant tone that I didn't want to know, as if somehow not hearing what he said would make it null and void. "Don't tell me! Don't tell me!" I began to scream while tears streamed down my face. Then, after refusing to be told again, I thought maybe I had heard him wrong, so now I needed to know what exactly what was going on. "Tell me! Tell me!" was the demand I now made of my distraught visitors. Sizani Khumalo whispered as gently as she could, "It's true, Lily. Bella is with us no more."

My heart shattered into a million pieces as the devasting news could no longer be denied. Tears fell like a waterfall from my eyes, and I sank to the ground. I was oblivious to the world outside my pain. I am sure the women all tried to comfort me, but I had no awareness of anything outside that big black hole of emptiness in my soul.

Stuart checked the time. It was 10.35 p.m., and the border at Lobatse closed at 12 a.m. (All others were already closed.) There was no time to waste. Tandy was alone in Pretoria. We had to get to Tandy to break the awful news about her sister before she heard it from someone else. Stuart grabbed an overnight bag and threw in an assortment of clothing for both me and him. I vaguely knew what he was doing but was still numb and deep in shock. I heard Stuart tell the three visitors the plan, and at the mention of Tandy's name, I instantly came back to reality. Yes, we had to go. We had to get to my other daughter as fast as we could, and then we needed to find out the terrible truth about what happened to our beautiful Bella.

Once I was loaded in the car with the meagre luggage, Stuart drove off, leaving the Khumalos to return to their homes in their own time. It was the beginning of the worst journey of my life. I tried to be strong, but every ten minutes or so, the grief came pouring out in uncontrollable sobs. Stuart, of course, was hurting too, but he remained focused on the task of getting us to the border before it closed.

We arrived at Pioneer Gate Border Post with just minutes to spare. As I handed my passport over to the immigration officer, I collapsed and ended up as a heap on the floor. I am sure Stuart saw me, but for some reason, he did not come to my rescue. I slowly pulled myself up and retrieved the passport and then headed out the door back to the car with no words spoken.

It would take at least four hours to reach the commune where Tandy lived in Hatfield, Pretoria. Stuart and I travelled mostly in silence as the Pajero sped towards its destination. I was still in shock, and my mind had become locked on one thought only: I have lost my big, baby girl. Just when it seemed as if I had used up all my tears, some more drops escaped, trickling slowly down my face.

About 40 kilometres outside of Pretoria, my faithful vehicle started losing power. We eventually had to stop on the side of the road in the middle of nowhere so that Stuart could investigate the problem. He opened the bonnet and peered inside, hoping to see something recognisably wrong that could be fixed. Nothing was evident in the darkness, so the next step was to call the AA (Automobile Association) for assistance. Unfortunately, we were told that it was not part of their jurisdiction to attend to vehicle breakdowns. Stuart sighed in despair that he would have to wait until the sun came up to get a proper look at the engine and diagnose the fault. He adjusted our seats so that we could try to get some sleep in the meantime. He succeeded in just a few minutes, but I remained fully awake, despite being emotionally exhausted.

As I lay on the reclined car seat, I became conscious of my heart beginning to beat irregularly. "Oh, no, not palpitations!" I murmured to myself. The last thing I needed was to have a full-on attack and end up in hospital. We had to get to Tandy! I began to self-counsel. "Keep calm. You are going to be fine." Somehow, I convinced myself that all was well, and beat by beat, my heart responded until it returned to a normal rhythm. My mission was now to relax and avoid the onset of an anxiety attack, which would make the nightmare even more frightening. I still couldn't sleep, but I lay there motionless so that I didn't disturb my driver's slumber.

After thirty minutes or so, I gently woke Stuart up. It was 5 a.m., and Tandy would be waking up to the worst news of her life. He looked inside the bonnet of the Pajero again, but there was no visible clue as to why the car had lost power. "Let's drive at a low speed. We will still get to Pretoria. We need to get there before Tandy wakes up," I reasoned. We then set off again and trundled slowly down the road like a tortoise with a hangover to avoid overstraining the engine.

When we arrived at the commune, there was no sign of anyone being awake. Everyone was fast asleep, including Tandy. I tried calling her on the phone so that she could unlock the main door and let us in, but there was no answer. Fortunately, the caretaker, who must have been at the back of the property, had heard the vehicle pull up and came to investigate. After we gave him a brief explanation, the caretaker at last enabled us to enter the building. Tandy opened the door of her room still half asleep—it was going to be a very rude awakening, but it had to be done.

The awful words tumbled out of my lips in unison with the tears streaming down my face. Tears fell immediately from Tandy's eyes too, but she was calm and hugged me tightly. "Oh, Mum, you have lost your daughter. I am so sorry," Tandy cried gently. She did not focus on her own great loss but on consoling her broken mother. I was struck by her selflessness and compassion. It gave me the strength that I needed to pull myself back together into one piece. Stuart also helped me return to rational thinking by declaring that I should contact Musa so that we could find out what had happened to our daughter.

Musa's voice was subdued and barely audible. He was on the way to the police station in Bronkhorstspruit, close to where Bella's body had been found. He was in search of the same answers that we were looking for. I informed Musa that we would meet him at the police station. Stuart said he knew the place, which was about 50 kilometres east of Pretoria. Tandy was already dressed and ready to leave, so we set off. Tandy and I held hands in the back seat with tears escaping sporadically but with brave, though false, smiles on our faces.

When we were just about a few kilometres from our destination, Musa called to say he was already there and that we should not come to the station, as he would deal with everything. I stated firmly that we were just about to arrive and I needed to be there. On our arrival, Musa introduced us to Detective Lombard, who was in charge of the case. All the police knew at this stage was that Bella appeared to have been strangled, and Lombard was determined to find out who was to blame. The detective revealed that he had a daughter of a similar age and said that he felt our pain.

We were asked to sit down while Lombard asked both Musa and me questions about Bella's recent communications and where she had been over the last few days. I reported that I had received an email message from Bella sent on Wednesday afternoon but had not been able to reach my daughter since then. The detective explained that her body had been found on an empty plot a few metres away from a gravel road on Saturday morning. Some hired workers had been starting to clear the plot so the owner could lay the foundations for his house, and in the process, they'd made the shocking discovery.

It looked like Bella must have been abducted and then left for dead at the remote spot. I could not make sense out of why Bella would put herself in such a position that she could be kidnapped. She had been found with her handbag and overnight bag, as if she were visiting someone, but my daughter would never have gotten into a stranger's car. She was far too sensible, and her experience in Johannesburg with the robbers had certainly made her aware of the presence of criminals in South Africa. So, even if Dumisani was right and she had been on her way to see her "new boyfriend", Bella would have taken a proper taxi to the bus station or gotten a lift from a friend who she knew well. It just didn't add up somehow.

We were then told that one of us needed to identify the body to make sure it was indeed our daughter. Musa immediately stood up, and his girlfriend followed suit. She held his arm as they followed Lombard's directions to where the body lay. Sibongile had been my ex-husband's partner for some time by then, and although I knew she was a reserved and gentle woman, I witnessed that she was also very supportive of Musa. The couple disappeared into the passageway leading to the room. I got up from my chair with the intention of following them, but I was suddenly filled with dread and sank back down on the seat. "I can't do it," I sobbed, "It's too hard!"

I have never regretted that decision. My memory of my beautiful daughter remains more or less intact. I already knew in my soul that Bella was gone. I didn't need to see her lifeless body and suffer more pain. When Musa emerged from the passage, his head was in his hands, and he cried, "They have beaten my baby!" Sibongile quickly came to his rescue and held him close, even though she was crying too. "Don't go in there, Lily!" Musa sternly advised. I assured him that I could not see Bella like that. I felt his pain, and it magnified my own. But again, I was aware that I needed to keep calm, as my heartbeat was threatening to go out of control.

Once the formalities had been completed at the police station, Detective Lombard announced that the next step was to go to the flat where Bella had been living and question the security guards. I was pleasantly surprised when he invited us to go with him, as he could have had the view that we would get in the way of his investigation. I guess he understood that for all of us, sitting and waiting to hear some information would have been absolute hell. Taking action gave us purpose and something to fill the void that Bella's death had created. My only mission at that time was to find out what had happened to our girl, so I didn't think twice about accepting the invitation, and neither did the rest of our troop.

At Lynwood Manor flats, we all alighted from our vehicles but let the detective and his officers go ahead and question the security guards on duty. They checked their records, and Lombard told us that there was an entry of Bella coming into the flats on Thursday afternoon but nothing to suggest she had ever gone out. It was possible that the guard on duty could have somehow missed her leaving, but he was now off duty, so he was not available to corroborate this information.

The detective went upstairs to the second floor flat, and Musa followed. They were unable to get in, as it was locked and a warrant would be needed to break into Dumisani's flat. However, Musa told us that he saw a duvet hanging over the railing inside the flat, signifying it had been recently washed. Musa already firmly believed that Dumisani was behind Bella's murder, but I felt that there must be some other explanation. After all, Dumisani still loved his ex-fiancée, and I could not comprehend him doing such a terrible thing as strangling her.

Other people started arriving at the flats. Musa's half-brother joined us, followed by the girls' cousins, Bonolo and Thapelo Malinga. The news of Bella's untimely demise had started to spread amongst the family members living in the area, and they naturally needed to know more and to be there to support us. During this time, I was in a daze, still unable to fully take in the scenario unfolding in front of my eyes. Or maybe it was just a defence mechanism to protect my heart and my soul from emotion that could easily spiral out of control.

More vehicles pulled into the car park at the flats. A young, white South African man approached me looking very puzzled. "Are you Isobel's mother?" he asked, which told me that he must know her in order to deduce that possibility. I answered in the affirmative, and Jack introduced himself as a close friend of Steven, Bella's long-standing acquaintance. His buddy had sent him to check on Bella; he was worried about her well-being, as she had not turned up at his place the night before. Steven was not comfortable coming in person, as Dumisani had made it very clear previously that he was not welcome at the flat and he didn't want to create any problems.

I had no choice but to utter the heart-breaking words "Isobel is dead". Jack was clearly shocked, however he remained calm and composed. I explained that we were at the flats to ascertain what had happened to Bella and that we needed to contact Dumisani so that he could hopefully give us further information. Jack, as it turned out, was actually a friend to both Steven and Dumisani. Without saying a word, he took out his cell phone and put it on redial.

"Hi, Dumisani. Isobel's mum would like to talk to you."

After a pause, he handed the phone over to me. I had no chance to pre-plan what I was going to say. I asked Dumisani where he was, and he replied that he was in Pretoria North at a friend's house. I told him that I was at the flat looking for Bella and needed to see him urgently. Dumisani queried whether he should come to the flat, and

I confirmed that it was exactly what I wanted him to do. Dumisani agreed and said he would come there as soon as he had organised transport. I thanked him for his cooperation and handed the phone back to Jack.

By then, we had been joined Musa and some of his relatives. I recounted the phone conversation and was advised to inform the detective about what had just transpired, as Lombard was keen to question Dumisani. The initial plan was just to wait for Dumisani's arrival, but after some twenty minutes, Jack decided to call again to ensure that he was on his way to us. Dumisani said he had now gotten a car and was just about to leave. Nothing had been said about Bella being deceased, but Dumisani seemed to realise that it was important for him to keep to his word. However, Musa doubted that Dumisani would come to the flat. He was convinced that Dumisani was guilty of the crime. I reasoned to myself that if Dumisani had had anything to do with Bella's death, then he would have already run away. Also, when I'd spoken to him the day before, he'd showed no hint of being traumatised.

Musa dictated that we should all leave the flats, as Dumisani was not going to turn up, and that we should let the police do their work. It must have been past lunchtime by then, though no one felt like eating. Still, Stuart and I needed to find somewhere to stay, so we left, and the others followed suit.

Our natural choice of where to stay was with our good friends, the Thompsons, who lived in Johannesburg. Although it was an hour's drive from Pretoria, we had stayed in their home many times before, both at their present house and in Bloemfontein. Unfortunately, this was not a good time for the Thompsons to have visitors. Mr Thompson had just been diagnosed with life-threatening cancer, and they were coming to terms with the shock, so we felt that they did not need the added stress of our trauma. It was Stuart's ex-wife who came to the rescue and volunteered to accommodate us at her home in the outskirts of Johannesburg before we had even thought of the possibility. We arrived at Adele's house late in the afternoon, and there were hugs and tears on both sides. This became the ritual every time I reunited with someone new for the days, weeks, and months to follow.

The big question of what had happened to our darling daughter was still unanswered, and to be honest, I was too numb and too broken to try to comprehend the reality of the situation. We were offered drinks while food was being prepared, and I sipped a glass of wine drop by drop. It was then that we could open the floodgates to allow the bombardment of phone calls to come through, as we were in a position to answer. I had called my brother in the United Kingdom before we'd left our house in Botswana and delivered the news of Bella's death to his wife, who had answered. There'd been silence for some minutes after that delivery while Angela had slowly come to terms with my words. Now, after our arrival at Adele and Brian's place, Angela was one of the first people to reach out to us.

Members of the Khumalo family started to arrive after establishing our whereabouts. It was comforting to talk with Bonolo, Bella's cousin, as she has been so close to me since her own mother was murdered some years back. Our kind host offered us food, but I struggled to eat even a little of the braaied meat and salads. Both Stuart's phone and my own continued to ring almost continuously, so we were fortunate that Adele and others took over the duty answering them unless the caller was someone very close to the family.

Bella's heartbroken friends also managed to track us down and began arriving at the house. I knew it would be hard for them to come to terms with losing a truly great and genuine friend. I was determined to stay strong for them while they unburdened themselves of their pain. And then a young man entered the house with Jack. It had to be Steven. Even though I had not seen his face before, his deep sadness made him instantly recognisable.

I beckoned Steven away from the others, and we sat at the dining room table. As he introduced himself, tears escaped from his blue-green eyes. I held both his hands and tried to reassure him that everything would be all right. Steven was convinced that it was his fault that Bella had been killed by her ex-fiancé. I told him that we didn't even know if that was true and, in any case, he should not blame himself for another's actions. Steven was compelled to tell me the whole story of his love for my daughter. I listened intently and fought back my own tears. He had been in love with Bella from the first time he had met at her at the university. They'd been on similar degree courses and had spent time together in some of their joint classes. They had happily studied and chatted together outside of class too, but he'd been aware of Bella's commitment to her boyfriend in Botswana. Steven told me that during their conversations, they had invariably finished each other's sentences—that is how connected they'd been from the start.

However, after the first year was over, Steven gave up on his course and his relationship with Bella, as there seemed no future for him with either of them. He'd gone back to the United Kingdom to follow his original passion of becoming a game ranger. Steven had kept in touch with Bella, but just as distant friends would do. He'd completed the two-year training, and around the time he'd finished, he'd heard that Bella was no longer with her long standing boyfriend. This was the opportunity for which he had been secretly waiting. Steven had packed his bags and come back to South Africa to stay with his mother in Johannesburg, intending to find work and, more importantly, resume his relationship with Bella but now on another level.

Shortly after arriving back, Steven had hurried to the flat where Bella had been staying and had gotten a rude awakening. There had been a big omission in her communications with him. Bella was now engaged, and it had been her fiancé who had opened the door, not her! After a few awkward minutes, Bella had arrived at the door behind her fiancé, trying to keep her own surprise (and delight) at bay. She'd introduced Steven as her ex-classmate, and in return, he had explained that he'd been in the neighbourhood and had just come by to say hi. Whether Dumisani had accepted this explanation or not, Steven was not sure, but seeing Bella again had appeared to be no longer an option—that was, until she'd contacted him out of the blue to tell him that the engagement was off. Bella had not been open to discussing what had happened, so the conversation had been diverted to a music festival taking place in Johannesburg two weeks from then. Steven had been happy to invite Bella to stay with him at his mother's place so that they could attend the festival together.

Little did Steven know that it would be the last time that he would see his beloved Isobel alive. They'd had such a great time that weekend that Bella had been reluctant to return to Pretoria. She had been adamant that she'd wanted to stay another day, even if it meant missing a class. Bella had told Steven that she would arrange someone to take notes for her and would easily catch up on what she had missed. When Bella had finally left on Tuesday morning, she had assured Steven that she would be back Friday night. However, on that night, Steven had received an uncharacteristic message from Bella saying that she wanted to spend some time on her own and would not be visiting him after all. Later on, I found out that Tandy had received a similar message from her sister, as they'd often spent Friday nights together, and Tandy had also thought the content of the message was a bit strange. After hearing nothing further from Bella during Saturday, Steven had sent Jack to investigate and had been hit by the heartbreaking news.

With this part of the story released from his lips, Steven put his head in hands and wept. I think it was only few minutes after talking to Steven that I received an urgent call to my phone. The caller was Dumisani!

The shaky voice at the other end of the line asked me what was going on. Dumisani said the police had been questioning him and now wanted to take him to the police station under arrest. For some unknown reason, he had decided to call me for an explanation. I simply told him that he was probably the last person to see Bella alive, so it was logical that they would need to question him further. I answered him truthfully, as I still had not reached the conclusion that he had had anything to do with my daughter's death. Shortly afterwards, I heard that Musa had also called on the house phone to tell us that the police had informed him that Dumisani had been arrested. Musa, unlike me, was now completely convinced of Dumisani's guilt.

Eventually, the visitors left, and the phones were put on silent so that we could get some sleep. I had not slept on Saturday night during our challenging road trip to Pretoria and thus was completely and utterly exhausted. It was only that exhaustion which enabled me to finally drift off to sleep, despite my mind going over and over all that had happened since the bombshell had been dropped on my soul.

When I awoke in the morning, reality came rushing in. I kept quiet, but I was sliding down into a deep abyss and might never to return to daylight. Stuart jumped out of bed and announced that he would make us coffee as if it were a normal Monday morning. I don't think I answered, as I was overcome with a dark despair. I thought to myself, *There is no point in getting out of this bed. I don't want to live without my Bella!* Tears of hopelessness streamed down my face. Life no longer had any meaning.

Through my damp eyes, I suddenly became aware of a light on the wall. I sat up. The light seemed to have escaped through a gap in the curtains, and yet it was heart-shaped and appeared to pulsate. I felt Bella's presence, and in my mind, she said, *Mummy, you have to forgive him. I have forgiven him. I want you to live. You have to live. I love you!* I knew she was right. I felt myself fly up out of that black, bottomless pit like Superman on a mission, and as I arrived at the top, the heart-shaped light pulsated one final time and disappeared.

I got out of bed in a bewildered daze and pulled back the curtains to be met with a solid brick wall! The angelic light could not possibly have come from outside. There was no doubt in my mind —it had been Bella's spirit speaking to me. My inner strength was instantly renewed, and as Stuart opened the door, I indicated that I would drink the coffee with my hosts, not hidden away in the room. I mentioned nothing of the experience to him, as I knew he did not believe in such things and was not interested in learning about the spiritual realm. For Stuart, life was just a short journey on earth, and that was all there was until it came to an end.

Both Musa and Bella's spirit were correct. We got a call from Detective Lombard during the morning stating that Dumisani had confessed to the murder. The boy said that he'd taken Bella's life in his flat on Thursday afternoon but had only removed her body on Friday evening. Apparently, Dumisani's parents had visited him at his cell in the police station, but the visit had turned sour. Dumisani must have admitted the truth to them, expecting support, but instead, his father had walked away, saying that Dumisani was no longer his son and that he wanted nothing further to do with him. This abandonment had led to Dumisani spilling the beans to the detective in the morning. He could no longer rely on his father's position as a magistrate to protect him. If anything, his position had the opposite effect.

Lombard explained that the details of my daughter's death were yet to be established, but they had already started to interrogate Dumisani. I guess it was a kind of relief to at least have a major part of the puzzle solved. My mind was now going over the phone calls from Dumisani. In fact, I began to examine his whole relationship with my daughter for answers. Why had he killed her? Why hadn't I known that things were so bad between them? How could he have been driven to do such a thing? Why, oh, why had this happened to my beautiful, clever girl?

We all descended on the police station in Bronkhorstspruit, each of us with similar unanswered questions. At this stage, the detective's focus was on whether Dumisani's confession was indeed true. Dumisani had been asked where exactly he had taken Bella's body on Friday night, and the police had gone with him to verify the place. Although Bella's handbag, overnight bag, and shoes had already been removed as evidence, Dumisani was able to point out something they had missed. Behind a bush was Bella's black jacket, yet to be discovered. He was telling the truth about his terrible crime.

Chapter 10

Apart from gaining insight into what had transpired over the past few days, we also needed to start planning the way forward. Discussing funeral arrangements together with my ex-husband was something neither of us had ever envisaged, but that's what we did. I was clear in my mind that my wishes should take priority over his, after all, who had brought Bella up and cared for her all these years? I need not have worried, as Musa and his mother, Gwen, accepted without question that Bella's body should be cremated, even though their Christian preference would have been a burial. On my part, I had no problem with having a Christian service before the cremation. We agreed that Gwen and Musa would organise a pastor and other aspects of the service. Musa also categorically stated that he would take care of all the costs, which I really appreciated, given my financial situation at the time.

The service took place a few days later, after the autopsy had been performed. Most of the people who attended were relatives and friends of the Khumalo family, as it was too far and too short notice for people from our side of the family to come. In any case, Bella's secondary school and university had already started to make arrangements for a memorial service to be held the following week, enabling many more people to be invited, including her classmates, teachers, and lecturers.

Stuart, Tandy, and I had managed a quick trip back home to collect suitable clothing for the services and leave instructions with our house and farm workers for taking care of everything, including feeding our pets. We didn't alert our friends that we were in Ruretse for the day, as otherwise we would have been inundated with well-meaning visitors. This would not only have been emotionally draining but would have prevented us from making a speedy return to Pretoria. Only our next-door neighbours were aware of our secret visit, as we needed to ask them to keep an eye on our home during our absence.

The Christian service took place at the crematorium situated close to the police station in Bronkhorstspruit. Although wearing black was not compulsory at such a service, we all chose to do so. It reflected the heaviness of everyone's mood. I made a subconscious decision to be strong throughout the services for my daughter. If I fell apart like I had at the funeral for Musa's sister, Nothando, who was also murdered, then what hope would there be for everyone else to be stable. Few words were exchanged before the service started—it was too painful for small talk, and we all knew why we were gathered together at that solemn place. The only person to speak was the pastor, who had kindly agreed to lead the service at very short notice.

I thought the pastor would preach about God's role in our lives and deaths, but instead, he spoke on a very apt topic: forgiveness. It was not what I had expected, and I listened intently to the message he delivered loud and clear. The pastor explained the importance of forgiving a person guilty of such an ungodly deed as taking another's life. "If we don't forgive them, then we will be perpetuating the same ill feeling that led to the death of our beloved. We need to stop the cycle of not forgiving so that Isobel's death is not in vain," he said. I remembered again the words uttered by Bella's spirit begging me to forgive Dumisani as she had done. Yes, I forgave him.

Detective Lombard attended the service and met us briefly beforehand to give me the items Bella had had in her possession at the time of her death. Amongst them was the silver link bracelet that she had worn since I'd presented it to her for her eighteenth birthday. I immediately put it on—I needed her close to me during the ordeal of saying goodbye. I also had a small, white angel made of some sort of translucent plastic. I still don't remember who gave it to me, but I am very grateful that they did. I clutched that angel throughout the three services, and it somehow contributed to my inner strength.

Arrangements for the second service were taken care of by St Mary's DSG and Pretoria University (Tuks). The memorial service was to be held at the end of the week in the chapel that was part of St Mary's, with the lecturers and fellow students from Tuks being fully involved in the preparations. While that was going on, we had the difficult task of removing Bella's possessions from the flat.

Well, I said "we", but in fact, Stuart and Tandy refused me entry into the flat. The Pajero was parked around the corner from the flat under a big, old tree, and I was instructed to stay safely on its back seat. I couldn't see what was transpiring a few metres away, so there was nothing to focus my attention on. The only thing to do was to talk to the tree about my determination to be strong and keep my emotions under control. The solid trunk seemed to agree with my stance, and together we stood tall, with only the odd tear forcing itself to the surface.

After thirty minutes, Stuart came back. He needed to move the vehicle closer to the flat, as the belongings were now packed and were ready to transfer to the trailer and boot of the car. He parked the Pajero near the staircase, and I watched Stuart and Tandy going up and down with large boxes and some small pieces of furniture. But they were not the only ones carrying items on the staircase. Two women had decided to remove what belonged to Dumisani on the same day as us. I thought to myself that one of them must be his mother, and in that same moment, a woman knocked on the window. I opened it, and she asked if she could join me in the back of the car.

As the woman introduced herself, she cried that she was so sorry about what her son had done. "I brought him up the best I could, to be a decent Christian. I took him regularly to church. I don't understand why …" she exclaimed before she broke down into violent sobs. I don't know where my response came from—it must have been somewhere deep in my soul—but I calmly replied that it would be all right and that I hoped one day Dumisani would be able to forgive himself and do good in the world. We embraced, and peace flooded into both our hearts.

I met Dumisani's father at the memorial service a few days later, although I didn't realise it was him at the time. I had thought that maybe his mother would attend the service but had not expected him—after all, he wanted nothing to do with his son and the crime he had committed. After the service, refreshments were laid out in the chapel's courtyard, people had an opportunity to pay their respects to the family members, which of course included myself. A well-groomed gentleman approached me with an entourage behind him, indicating that he was someone important. He shook my hand as he offered his sincere condolences. Mr Masondo stated his name, but I didn't recognise it. Even when Mr Masondo mentioned that he had sent a letter to my ex-husband, I genuinely didn't know what he was talking about. It was only when Musa remarked that Dumisani's father had sat in front of him at the service that the penny finally dropped.

Returning to the emptying of the flat, I did enter the murder scene, despite my family's attempt to prevent it and to shield me from the pain of reality. Packing and removing Bella's possessions had taken several hours, and I needed to use the bathroom. I climbed the stairs and entered through the open door, determined to focus on getting out of the flat as quickly as possible. The flat consisted of one large room plus a bathroom. My eyes swept around the room as I rushed to my destination. Once inside, I found myself facing Bella's powder-blue dressing gown, which I had bought her many years ago. I grabbed the gown and clutched it close to my chest as I made my escape to the stairs. Shortly afterwards, we left the complex with a fully loaded vehicle and with very little conversation between the three of us. Then, at Adele and Brian's house, everything was squashed into their garage until we could take them back to Botswana.

The second service, which was a memorial service, was on the afternoon of Friday, 28 September. It was mainly organised by Bella's ex-classmates and their teachers and lecturers with a little input from the Granger, Khumalo, and Malinga families. We arrived early at the chapel, before any of the guests, which gave us a chance to find out more about the proceedings and meet those involved with the program. I was the only one from our family with a speech prepared, while Bonolo, Bella's cousin, was to speak on behalf of the Khumalo and Malinga families. There were representatives from the two institutions that Bella had attended, and one of her ex-colleagues provided beautiful music on her violin as the ceremony began.

The seats in the chapel rapidly filled, apart from those at the very front. Those seats were probably thought to be reserved for immediate family, but we were all seated elsewhere. People just kept arriving, and they soon had to stand at the back of the chapel and even outside in the foyer. Everything about the service was beautiful, from the flowers that adorned the chapel to the background melodies to the heartfelt speeches. When my turn came on the program, I was ready. I had kept cool and calm so far with no tears. I knew I needed to be composed to deliver those words.

While I spoke of my undying love for my daughter, the rest of my family stood behind me. It was good that I did not see the expressions or tears on their faces, as I surely would have broken down. Stuart, at one point, put his hand on my shoulder, but he was not able to do much more. I looked forward at all the people who loved Bella, and in that, I found my comfort. Whenever I wavered, I gripped the translucent angel in my hand harder and glanced at the silver bracelet. I would be strong for my Bella.

Bonolo's moving tribute to her cousin followed mine. It was sincere but with moments of humour that reminded us what a fun-loving girl dear Bella had been. There was only one part of the programme that melted my outwardly solid exterior. A close friend of Bella's from St Mary's played the piano while she sang a song that I had never heard before by Martina McBride. Her voice was soulful and crystal clear. "You can love someone with all your heart, for all the right reasons, and in a moment they can choose to walk away. Love 'em anyway." These words resonated with my heart and represented the missing piece of the jigsaw of my healing. There was a point to loving my daughter so deeply, even though she had been taken so cruelly away from me. Experiencing that love was the reward. Love anyway.

Looking back now, I would say that this was one of my biggest life lessons. No person, no creature, no possession, will be with us forever, but that does not mean we should hold back on love for fear of losing it one day. If anything, the opposite is true. Love fiercely and deeply. Tell those you love your true feelings towards them at every opportunity. Feel love and express love. As the saying goes, "It is better to have loved and lost then never to have loved at all." Ironically, you don't actually "lose" love. It will still be there, tucked away safely in your heart. It is there for you to connect with anytime the flow of love is needed in your veins. So, love anyway.

After the service, everyone made their way to the chapel courtyard, which was strewn with cream-white rose petals like angel tears. I soon had a long queue of people in front of me, waiting to offer condolences. Some had travelled long distances to be there. Philip, or Macky, as he was known, had driven with his wife all the way from Francistown at the northern end of Botswana. He had also picked up another good friend, Edwin, on the way in the capital Gaborone. I could see how hard it was for Macky to approach me. He broke down in tears, and I hugged him tight to console him but also to hold myself together. It was comforting to be on the receiving end of so much compassion and empathy, even from those I hardly knew (including Mr Masondo). I was particularly moved by the large presence of Bella's teachers and lecturers, not to mention her classmates and friends.

It was decided by a group of Bella's close friends and younger relatives that we should go to the Flair after the service. The local bar and meeting place used to be popular with Tuks students, and Bella used to go there regularly. I suggested to Stuart that we should go there too—after all, we needed to relax a little after the tension of the heart-wrenching service.

The hangout was a small place, and the after-memorial group more or less filled it. Steven was there with his mother, and it was good to chat with her and get to know the woman who could have been Bella's mother-in-law. Nothando's children, Bonolo and Tshepo, kept Tandy company, and it was comforting to hear them laugh and enjoy being together despite the occasion. Musa did not join us. I am not sure why, but he probably would have felt out of place, since he didn't know most of Bella's friends. After a while, one of those friends, Palesa, told me that there was a girl who wanted to talk to me. Palesa didn't know the girl, who was wearing dark glasses, but had been asked to convey the message to me.

I moved through the group to where the mysterious girl was sitting silently in the corner on her own. She looked up and beckoned for me to sit down next to her. She smiled and told me that her name was Christine. She then explained that she hadn't known Bella, as she was studying at Rhodes University, but had heard about the tragedy that had befallen my daughter. Christine went on to offer her sympathy at my loss and said that if I didn't mind, she really needed to tell me something important. I asked Christine to continue. The story that Christine related had me listening intently.

Christine's boyfriend had been regularly abusing her psychologically and physically, but she had put up with it until a few months before then because she loved him. Christine told me that she'd kept her mother in the dark about her boyfriend's behaviour until one day when he went too far. This man had taken a knife, slashed Christine's leg in anger, and then fled. The cut had been deep. Christine had gotten into a bath of water to somehow deal with the flowing blood, but it had been a serious cut, and she had begun to fade. Fortunately, her cell phone had been nearby, and she'd managed to make a desperate plea to her mother for help. By the time Christine's mother had arrived, she'd been too weak to get out of the bath. Her mum had had to break the lock to get access to her daughter.

Now, six months later, Christine had not taken any action against her so-called boyfriend, but at least they were no longer together. However, there were some crucial points to her story that she wanted to share with me, which were the reasons why she had not told her mother prior to the attack about the ongoing abuse. This was something that I had gone over in my mind many times. Why hadn't Bella told me that her fiancé was abusing her? What had the barrier been to her letting me know? If I had known, I could have saved my daughter from her untimely death. I felt somehow responsible.

I should have realised something was very wrong. These were the thoughts that tormented my brain and caused me sleepless nights. Christine held the key to unlocking my self-inflicted suffering.

Slowly, Christine revealed her truth. "I didn't tell my mother about what he was doing to me because I wanted to show her that I was independent and could handle my own life without her help," she said. "But the main reason was that I love my mother so much that I did not want to worry her about the situation with my boyfriend." Christine's words nourished my soul, which was so hungry for answers. I felt a peace flood through me that I had not felt for a long time. The reason Bella had not told me what was happening was not that we were too distant. If anything, we were too close.

Blaming oneself is part of the grief journey, especially with the loss of a child. After all, one of the prime responsibilities of a parent is to protect their child from harm. If something happens to a child, one immediately asks, Where were the parents? Why didn't the parents stop this from happening? And so on. But the truth is that no one belongs to another person. Life is a result of multiple choices. No person can be held responsible for another's choice. Even if you follow someone else's advice to jump off a cliff, you are the one who makes the choice to take that leap! My daughter chose not to tell me that her boyfriend was abusing her or that he was demonstrating obsessive behaviour. If I had known, I would surely have advised Bella to get out of the relationship fast. However, she would still have had to make the choice whether to pack her bags or stay.

The next day, Stuart, Tandy, and I returned to Botswana. There was one more service for Bella that we needed to organise, and we had only a few days in which to accomplish the task. This was likely to be the memorial service with the largest attendance, and it was to be held at our plot in Ruretse on Saturday, 6 October 2012. Fortunately, many people came to our aid with the arrangements. The slab that remained from our house burning down was the ideal site on which to erect the huge marquee that my dear friend Melanie volunteered to provide, along with chairs, tables, tablecloths, and so on, from her hiring service. A few kilometres from our plot lived the owners of a huge printing and marketing firm, and they very kindly offered to design and print the programme for the service free of charge. We just needed to supply suitable photographs and text, including a beautiful poem written by Tandy. Then our next-door neighbour, Ann South, and other friends volunteered to make sandwiches and cupcakes, while another very close friend, Naledi, arrived from Thamaga early on the day of the service and helped with all the preparations. I really don't know what I would have done without the support and love from Naledi throughout that difficult day.

Requests had gone out earlier to relatives and to Bella's friends to send us any photo memories they had in their possession. These were to be used in the huge montage that Tandy was compiling of Bella's life and in a PowerPoint slide show which was to play before and after the service. The three photos that I had framed for Bella's funeral service in Bronkhorstspruit were also to be put on display, as well as three original pictures we borrowed from an amateur photographer from a photo shoot he had done with Bella. I say "borrowed", but after the event, he kindly donated the stunning photographs to us. They can now be found on the walls in my sitting room.

A Facebook page had been set up to disseminate information about the memorial service that had taken place in Pretoria, and we now used it to provide the details of the Botswana service. This was also used as a forum for well wishes from those who were unable to attend. Condolences appeared on my own Facebook page too, which enabled more people to know about our loss and the upcoming service. Of course, there was very little time for checking it during the lead up to the service, and when I finally opened my page, I was blown away by the many messages on my timeline and in Messenger—some from people I had never met before and have never met since.

I read and acknowledged messages from family and the closest of friends, while I left others to be read after the service. However, there was a very long message from a lady called Natasha which somehow demanded my attention. I think there may have been more than one message from this lady, which may have been part of why I was drawn to read what she had to say. Or maybe it was because I was hooked by the first line: "Lily, you don't know me, but I have to talk to you. I have to be with you at your daughter's service this Saturday." Apparently Natasha had lost a child herself, a baby only 6 months old, and she was filled with compassion for my own loss.

My brother and his wife arrived. It was the first time Angela had set foot in Botswana. The encounter at Sir Seretse Khama Airport was wrought with emotional tension, but Angela and I managed to hold back the tears until we were safely out of public eye. There were still a few days to go before the service, and we had no accommodation, so Tony and Angela booked a small but beautiful guest house in Phakalane, only a few kilometres away from our farm in Ruretse. Once safely inside the hotel room, the two of us hugged and cried as one in our joint sorrow. The last time my brother had visited had been when the house had burnt down, and now he had to witness his sister fall to pieces yet again. Before Tony and Angela went back to the United Kingdom, they vowed that their next visit to Botswana would be a happy one!

Those attending the service from South Africa were mostly relatives of the Khumalo family. They made their own accommodation arrangements for the night before the service. Gwen, Bella's grandmother, and her two daughters, Anele and Sizani, all lived in Gaborone at that time, and thus other family members were able to stay with them. Darren and his mother were unable to join us, but they had attended the memorial in Pretoria. Meanwhile, a number of Bella's close friends, including Steven, arrived on the day of the service and brought tents to put up on our lawn. I don't think they used in them the end, as they didn't do much sleeping that night.

The morning of Saturday, 6 October 2012, was beautiful and bright. My birthday had been three days before, but it was the non-event of the year. All that occupied my mind was the loss of my much-loved daughter and the final service to celebrate the life I had shared with her. A large number of people were expected, so three hundred chairs had been positioned inside the huge marquee. However, those chairs filled up very rapidly, and some of the guests had to stand at the sides or at the back of the tent for over forty minutes. The service did not take very long, as it was a tribute to a wonderful human being rather than a religious ceremony. Bonolo Malinga was the master of ceremonies this time, and the prayer was read by my buddy, Annika, who had lived and worked with me during my early Gaborone High School days. If I remember rightly, I was the only parent who spoke about Bella. Her father and stepfather were lost for words. Tandy read the beautiful poem dedicated to her sister that was printed in the programme:

> *She's in the wind, you know; that's why it keeps on blowing.*
> *She's finally getting to see the places she always planned on going.*
> *She's in the water, you know; nothing could be more true.*
> *When there's not a cloud in sight, see her in the dew.*
> *She's in the sun, you know; that's why it keeps on shining,*
> *Every morning she rises, and you know there's no defeat in dying.*
> *She's in the sky, you know, and even though it seems to fall,*
> *Because you know she is everywhere and yet nowhere at all.*

After Tandy recounted some lovely and touching memories of her sister, various members of the Khumalo family spoke, and again Bonolo managed to inject some humour into the proceedings. My dear sister-in-law Angela read out the messages from those unable to attend from the United Kingdom, Canada, and New Zealand. The only time I was brought to tears was when my brother addressed me in his speech. He stated that I was a wonderful sister and he couldn't understand why such a tragedy should befall a mother who loved her daughter so much. I had not felt that close to him for a long time. The final messages came from Bella's friends, and the common thread woven through them all was that she had been such a great companion, always supportive, always making their lives happier and lighter.

Then it was time to greet some of the people who had come to give my family and me support that day. As I stepped out of the marquee, a long queue started to form of familiar faces wanting to offer their personal condolences. I spent a few minutes with each one, but the line did not seem to get any shorter. If anything, it continued to grow into a never-ending snake. Eventually, I realised that I was tired of standing pinned to one spot. I looked around and was directed to a chair on the lawn, which I gratefully accepted as my new position until I was free to mingle with the guests.

I joined my ex-husband and some of his relatives so that we could console each other in our similar loss. Musa said after a while that he needed the bathroom, and I agreed to take him there. As we approached the house, it was evident that his real motive was an opportunity to release his emotions. As Musa cried in my arms, I gently reminded him that he had another daughter and that it was time he paid her some attention, as she also needed his love.

Musa and I returned to the garden and were met by the mysterious Natasha and her husband. We were so happy to meet each other, and we embraced, even though we were strangers. Musa continued on, while I stopped to hear the story of how Natasha nearly hadn't arrived at the farm. Her husband had been stung by a bee while driving. He had started to beat his chest to try to prevent the inevitable sting, and it had looked to his wife like he was having a heart attack! Apparently, her husband normally gets an allergic reaction to bee stings, so they almost had to turn around and go back home, but here they were. I didn't know at this point that this was going to be the start of a long and deep relationship with Natasha and her family.

The afternoon was swallowed up by many conversations, and although I didn't get to chat with everyone present, I was pleased that I at least managed to thank Mrs Chetty, my ex-boss, for being at the service despite being confined to a wheelchair. There were many of my ex-colleagues present too, including head teachers from other private schools. I only found out that some people had been there days after the service was over.

So, that was the last of the three memorial services for my daughter. With no formal gatherings to organise, things began to get back to some sort of normality. That was not necessarily a good thing, as the services had been a distraction from the reality that my life was moving forward without Bella being part of it. While I'd felt I had no choice but to be strong with so many people around, I now had the luxury of being able to fall apart unobserved. And from time to time I did exactly that. Grief came in waves. Sometimes it was a gentle wave that caused a few tears to trickle down my face, while at other times, the waves would come crashing down, reducing me body and soul to a sobbing entity, hopelessly lost and broken.

Chapter 11

In the first few weeks after Bella's death, I had nights where I went to bed crying and woke up in the same state. Stuart did not attempt to comfort me. Maybe he thought I needed to let it all out, or maybe he was silently going through his own turmoil at the loss of his stepdaughter. I remember one night where I started to call my darling daughter's name. At first it seemed as though I expected her to respond, but with every repetition of "Bella", my voice became more desperate until I was literally screaming her name the top of my voice. I only stopped when I was so exhausted that I couldn't go on and was in danger of starting off an attack if I didn't calm myself down and accept reality.

Getting back to a routine was of great help. Not only did returning to my place of work require preparation and concentration, but the staff at the school provided the same support they'd afforded me when the house had burnt down. Minutes after entering my office, several teachers arrived and started to pray for my broken soul. There were hugs and assurances that I would get through this tragedy just like the last one. My soulmate, Rose, was constantly at my side. She did not need to say anything, as her presence was enough to make me feel loved and safe.

A phone call out of the blue also served to pull me out of the deep hole of grief. The caller asked if I was still holding a Christmas fair at the Eagle's Nest on 8 December, because this person wanted to hold a similar event on the same day. I had promised the Eagle's Nest management that I would organise the first market event on that date, and I had no intention of letting them or myself down. All of a sudden, I had lots to do to ensure that the fair would be a success. My passion took over from my grief. It was a stronger, positive emotion, and it automatically accelerated my healing.

Focusing on the positive aspects of my life and spending time with loving and compassionate friends certainly did a great deal towards hastening my recovery after this latest trauma. But what about Bella's spirit? I knew how my soul and heart were feeling, and yet had no idea of about hers. Was my daughter free from all pain? Was she at peace? Was she happy? I decided to do something I had never done before—enlist the help of a medium to get the answers I so badly needed from the spirit world.

Rose volunteered to accompany me to see Frank Dube, a recommended psychic medium, and I was very glad she did. After a short introduction, we two soulmates sat together on the couch to listen to Frank connecting with the spirit guides. I was surprised when he mentioned the names of the many angels watching over me. Some I vaguely recognised as relatives who had long ago left this planet, while others didn't ring any bells in my memory. Frank described an elderly man who was partially bald with some thin white hair and who had a well-built stature. He said this spirit wanted to talk to me, and his name was Charles. "That's my dad!" I exclaimed. I don't think I had told anyone in Botswana my father's actual name, so I knew Frank was not making it up. Frank continued to tell me that although Charles wanted to speak with me, he was aware that this was not his time—it was my daughter's.

Frank reported that his guide had contacted Bella's spirit. She was thrilled at the connection and wanted to give Rose and I a bunch of flowers each. Oh yes, Bella knew how much I loved flowers! I held Rose's hand tightly as a few tears ran down my face. Later, Rose revealed that she had cried the same tears. Then Bella conveyed something that has empowered and guided me since that day. I had asked Frank to find out what I could do for her. Bella's answer was simple: all she wanted was for her mother to be happy. If I could be happy, then she would be happy too. At last, there was some action I could take for my girl! I instantly felt stronger and was determined to achieve my new mission in life—a mission that was far from impossible. From then on, I was going to do my best to be happy.

I returned twice to Frank on my own after this first session, but it was the first meeting that had the greatest impact. On each occasion, though, I became more convinced of Bella's continued presence in my life. Frank mentioned events that I had not told anyone about. One morning, I had been awakened by a gentle knock on the front door of the cottage but had found no one outside. Bella's spirit claimed responsibility. Frank recounted the time when I had pulled my bedroom curtains closed and gotten into bed only to find them still open. I was not getting forgetful in my old age or going insane. Bella was trying to get my attention!

I learnt that it was no coincidence that Bella's full name, Isobel, had been my great-grandmother's name. They were one and the same spirit. This relative whom I had never met had chosen to come to me as my daughter to take care of me and learn the few lessons remaining for her spiritual development. No wonder Bella was wise beyond her years and our roles often seemed to interchange. This also explained why her time on earth was so short.

Frank told me that Bella was destined to leave this planet early, and that there were three possible ways that it could have happened. I instantly recalled the time when Bella had had a gun pointed directly at her face. The car she'd been in had been followed from Johannesburg airport, and as it had pulled into her friend's yard, they'd realised they had company. The gangsters' vehicle had gotten stuck in the automatic gate as it was closing, and they'd jumped out wielding guns. The thugs had threatened the lives of all the passengers to scare them into handing over all their valuables. When it had been Bella's turn, she'd handed over the bag on her lap, but her phone and another bag had remained hidden under her legs. She'd been cool headed, even in such a deadly situation. Bella, her friend, and her friend's family had gotten out the ordeal unscathed, but when she'd called me a day later to tell me what had happened, I'd still cried at the thought of my daughter being in such imminent danger.

Even if Bella had survived the attack by her ex-fiancé, she would not have survived a terrible car crash that would have happened in her early thirties. After hearing all this, I surrendered to the fact that

I had no power over Bella's fate and that her journey in this realm was ordained to be a short one.

During the third appointment, Frank concentrated on his role as a psychic, rather than as a medium, and gave me information on my future destiny. After a while, I asked him to go back to his other role and to connect me with my father, as there seemed to be some unfinished business between us. Eventually, we were in spiritual communication, and I was sure that I was going to receive an apology from my dad for the way he had treated my mother and for the tense atmosphere in our home during my visits in the later years.

As a result of doing a Journey process with a practitioner and dear friend, Annabel Wright, I had already forgiven my father, and now I suspected that his spirit needed to apologise to conclude the healing in our relationship. I had also found out about my dad's family history, which had helped me understand why he had behaved in such a negative way towards other people, but that did not excuse him from saying sorry. However, it was not an apology I got but something much more important.

"Charles says he wants you to know that he is happy. He is at peace," Frank channelled. I felt a pleasant tingling sensation as those words soaked in, and a smile come to my face. I remembered how sad my father had looked the last time I'd seen him alive. I had glanced up at his window as we'd gotten into the car and had seen him gazing down at us with a look that said, Am I ever going to see you again? So, Dad is all right now. That was a great relief and was all I really needed to know. That was my last session with Frank at his meditation centre, but I have met him many times in passing and am always greeted with a warm smile and a positive snippet on my daughter's presence in my life.

Chapter 12

By 2013, I had made substantial progress in my healing and was still actively taking responsibility to ensure that my grief did not detract from my overall happiness. I read books on forgiveness and joy; I watched online webinars and videos presented by people who had successfully dealt with their grief or who explained techniques for maintaining a positive and a happy outlook on life; and I started helping other women who had lost their own children, either before or after I lost mine. Giving support and advice to these women was of great benefit to me and hopefully to them. I have since understood that the counsel you give to others is often exactly what you need to hear yourself, as it comes from your own inner wisdom. When you light a candle for someone else, it also brightens the darkness around you.

There was still one major hurdle to get over in my journey of healing from losing my daughter—the murder trial. I had seen many murder trials on television, and one of my favourite series had been *Law and Order*, which featured both the murder investigation and the court case that followed. However, I had never imagined that I would have a role in a real-life investigation and trial. It took some months after Bella's death for the wheels of justice to turn through various preliminary meetings and the trial date to be set for July 2013.

On Valentine's Day, four months after Bella's murder, a celebrity was killed by her fiancé also in Pretoria. Unsurprisingly, the trial of Oscar Pistorius took centre stage. He was probably even more well-known than his victim, due to his amazing achievements as an athlete with two artificial legs. Oscar's beautiful fiancée, Reeva Steenkamp, had been shot through the bathroom door in the middle of the night. Oscar claimed that he had thought he was shooting at an intruder. His story held little water, but somehow his lawyer managed to outwit the state prosecutor. The trial dragged on for several months. The case was tried in the main courtroom at Pretoria's Gauteng High Court and may well have been a factor in the delay of our own trial.

Oscar's murder trial taking precedence over Dumisani's trial may have been a blessing in disguise. The media coverage that the case attracted meant that the killing of a fiancée (or ex-fiancée, in Bella's scenario) was a topic widely discussed and debated. There was outrage from many, especially Reeva's parents, over the leniency in Oscar's sentence. His disability had not stopped Oscar from killing Reeva in cold blood or from lying in court, and yet somehow, it was taken into consideration during his sentencing. At one point, it seemed that he was not going to see the inside of a jail cell at all! At the very least, we were all reminded that violence against women continued to go on unabated and that there was need for some stern deterrents to reduce it rapidly.

After several false starts, something actually happened in the courtroom for our case. I think Stuart was there with me in Pretoria for the first attempt at getting the case started, but from then on, he was working away from home on a big building project and thus unable to transport me to Pretoria. On a couple of occasions, I managed to get lifts from friends who were heading in the same direction at just the right time. I missed two of the hearing dates, leaving Tandy to attend on her own with friends and relatives of the Khumalo family, but I didn't miss anything either time.

The reasons why nothing took place in the courtroom on several of the prescribed dates were mostly that Dumisani's lawyer was not ready or just did not turn up. Later, we were told it was due to sudden illness. From my point of view, it appeared that psychological delaying tactics were being employed, as when the lawyer was not there, neither was Dumisani. When I did get to see Dumisani during the first court date, I felt nothing. I was devoid of emotion—no anger, no hatred, no compassion, just emptiness in my heart. This was the person who had prematurely ended my daughter's life, and yet he was a stranger to me. Maybe I had erased him from my memory so that I would not be vulnerable to the pain of seeing him with the memories that seeing him would dredge up. It was if Dumisani was part of someone else's story, not mine.

In September 2013, nearly a year after Bella's death, the courtroom proceedings finally got underway. At last, everyone was present, except Stuart and Nothando's children, who had taken many days off work already for the previous non-starter court dates. I sat with Tandy's close friend Laurie and friends of Bella, while Dumisani's relatives sat behind us. Musa was also there with his partner, Sibongile. Tandy was a witness for the state and thus was not allowed in the courtroom until called to give testimony. I didn't like her being on her own outside on the cold bench, but I knew she was strong enough to play the required role.

After the initial legal statements, Dumisani was asked to read his confession to the court. I listened intently, as this was how I was going to find out the details of what had happened to my beloved daughter, even if it was her murderer's version. Dumisani's account at least provided a timeline of the events that led up to him strangling Bella and what came afterwards. It was painful to hear Dumisani's words, but that pain was locked up inside a cage so that I could be fully attentive to his story.

Dumisani claimed that Bella had been unfaithful to him prior to this occasion and that this time was the final straw. However, he failed to point out that they were no longer in a relationship, and the state prosecutor deliberately left this out too, in case it would somehow jeopardise the case. Bella's fictional promiscuity was used to justify him losing control on that fateful Thursday afternoon when she came back to the flat. According to Dumisani, after the argument on Wednesday, Bella had left the flat, while he'd stayed there overnight. Instead of going to work the next day, he'd stayed in the flat, apparently needing to rest after a sleepless night. Dumisani could have left the flat at any time, but he had not. Later in the testimonies, we found out that a friend had come to the flat to take Dumisani out for a drink but that he'd declined the invite. In my mind, it was clear that Dumisani had been lying in wait for my daughter's return like a lion stalking its prey.

The charge made at the beginning of the hearing was premeditated murder, so the defence lawyer tried to make it appear that Dumisani had been under severe psychological distress, causing his "spontaneous action". It was the prosecutor's task to prove otherwise. It was shocking to hear from Dumisani that after killing Bella, he'd left her body in the flat and gone to a party with friends. He was even reported to have been in the company of a new female friend. Dumisani had only come back the next day in a car he had hired specifically to remove Bella's body from the flat—the same car which had given him away when he'd met the police that Sunday. It was even more shocking to find out that he'd spent the whole day in the flat with her corpse, waiting for it to get dark. Dumisani had then wrapped Bella's body in her duvet and carried it down two flights of stairs to place it in the boot of the car along with her handbag, coat, and overnight bag.

The rest of the story I already knew, but some of the details were almost unbelievable. Not only had Dumisani used Bella's credit card to pay for the car he'd hired and put petrol it, but he'd even had the audacity to use it to buy himself a burger and fries to eat on the journey out of town. Before he set off from the flat, he had also made use of Bella's phone to message her sister and Steven to say that she would not be visiting either of them that day, as she needed time on her own. When Tandy had gotten that message, she'd been surprised, as Bella had been very outgoing and always enjoyed company.

Information from Lombard's team disclosed that Bella's body had not been carefully deposited on the open ground where she'd later been found. There was evidence that it had been dragged along inside the duvet and that her belongings had been thrown in the bush randomly. Indeed, it had been Bella's coat that had confirmed that Dumisani was telling the truth about being the one who had abandoned my daughter's body at this site.

What I found the most disturbing was the coroner's report. The elderly gentleman was standing close to where I was sitting, and as he spoke, he was turning the pages of his records, which included graphic photographs of Bella that I really didn't want to see. The coroner stated that there had been bruising to Bella's face and chest which had been incurred before her death. As he referred the judge to the photographic evidence before him, the corner's own pictures caught my eye. Seeing Bella's lifeless and bruised face made me want to run out of the courtroom. Laurie sensed my uneasiness and asked if I wanted to leave. I muttered a feeble yes and started to get up from my seat, but I quickly changed my answer to a firm no, held Laurie's hand tightly, and sat back down.

After the glimpse of that photograph, I now understood why Musa had been so distraught after seeing Bella's body at the station and why he'd exclaimed that someone had beaten up his girl. It was concluded that the injuries had been caused at least a day before she'd been strangled. Dumisani claimed that Bella had attacked him during the argument on that Wednesday and he had merely defended himself from her blows.

The worse part of the report was yet to come. The coroner went on to explain that there was extensive damage to Bella's heart tissue due to the trauma it had gone through. Despite no oxygen entering her body, her heart had frantically tried to send some to her brain. I was not able to digest the meaning of this statement until some hours later. Maybe I was distracted by the corner's next bombshell, that Bella did not die immediately. If Dumisani had been truly remorseful, then he could have called emergency services, and maybe, just maybe, they could have saved my baby.

Tandy was called into the courtroom when the prosecutor was cross-examining Dumisani, and she brought up the incident when, sometime in August 2012, Bella had sought refuge at her sister's place. I had only heard about this episode after Bella's death. One evening, Dumisani had insisted on reading the messages on Bella's phone, and she had locked herself in the bathroom to escape his attack. While there, Bella had called the police, who had come to the flat and escorted her to Tandy's accommodation. This is what Tandy was asked to verify in her testimony. The aim was to show that Dumisani had demonstrated aggressive behaviour towards Bella previously, and thus, when he killed her, it was not out of the blue but something that was pre-planned and intentional.

Indeed, there was another story I had heard from one of Bella's friends, wherein she'd been with Dumisani at a party. He'd upset Bella somehow, and as a result, she'd thrown her drink in his face. He'd retaliated by putting his hands around her throat and had only been prevented from going further due to the social setting. This occasion was not brought up in court.

Neither Musa nor I had to take the stand, and the only other witness called was Herman, a mutual friend to both Bella and Dumisani. His role was to explain where he'd found Bella's phone, which had previously been reported as missing from the scene of the crime. Herman had spotted the phone in the back garden where he lived, next door to where Dumisani was staying temporarily in Pretoria North. It was established that Dumisani had thrown it there a day after the murder, realising it would be used as evidence against him if found in his possession.

When the case was adjourned, it was late afternoon. Tandy and I had had lunch with Musa and Sibongile earlier, and this time, we went our separate ways. Accompanied by Nothando's children and Bella's close friends, including Herman, we went to News Cafe in Hatfield Square, another popular hangout of university students. There was soft chatter around the table, which helped in redirecting our thoughts away from the harsh reality of the courtroom. We decided to treat ourselves to an assortment of colourful cocktails as another welcome distraction.

I sipped and listened to the young people's conversations. For once, I didn't feel like joining in with appropriate or witty remarks. I couldn't even taste the golden liquid rising up my straw. My mind was still back in the courtroom seeing flashes of Bella's photograph as the description of the condition of her heart continued to echo loudly. I felt like a desperate prisoner until something brushed lightly against my ankle. We were sitting in an enclosed restaurant, but there on the floor was a delicate, silver-grey feather. It was a message from Bella; she was setting me free from my self-imposed dungeon.

Tandy saw the look on my face and asked if I was all right. I instantly replied in the negative and jumped up from my seat to flee into the cool evening air. Tandy caught up with me in the middle of the courtyard and put her arm around my shoulders. I was breathing heavily, and I exclaimed that I couldn't stop thinking about the damage that had occurred to Bella's heart. Tandy gave me an explanation that stopped my runaway heartache in its tracks: "Of course she would try relentlessly to live. She didn't want to leave you!" It made sense. Yes, Tandy was right. Could I really have expected Bella not to try to hold on to dear life, regardless of the consequences to her body? Tears washed down my face. After a few minutes, I returned to the table, now able to face reality thanks to both of my daughters.

Part Four

Coming into Bloom: Loving Yourself into the Beautiful Being That You Are

As our true nature blossoms, our ego fears and defenses dissolve in the light of our love.

—Deepak Chopra.

Some plants take a long time to produce buds, let alone to flower, while others wither and die before getting that far. It is always exciting to see those we love reach that stage of finally opening up all their petals to radiate the beauty within them. Much may have taken place to get plants or loved ones to that place of glory. They may have had to survive harsh growing conditions, lack of water or sun, the onslaught of pests and diseases, or competition from relentless weeds. As any avid gardener knows, it is not easy to deal with all these challenges, but the prize is certainly worth it! Weeds, in particular, can do a lot of damage. They can slowly remove nutrients from the soil that the plant itself needs. Weeds can host pests and diseases which attack the plant, and they can block out the life-giving sun. Removing weeds is not a once-off task; it is something that needs to be done throughout the growing period. But eventually, they will be gone if we don't give up.

Each one of us has our own individual challenges, some more than others. Accepting what happens, forgiving others and ourselves, and letting go of what no longer serves us is all part of self-love, and it allows us to be happy and to bloom.

Chapter 13

The road of loss and grief is a long, rocky one with no end in sight. I was no stranger to this road, as the loss of my home and all its contents had provided me with a travel pack for the journey. The same emotions of devastation, sadness, anger, self-doubt, guilt, and hopelessness washed over and through me in the months and years after Bella's death. We are told that with time, the pain will lessen, the harsh memories will soften, and the fragmented heart will become stronger, and from my experience, this is true. However, this does not magically happen on its own. If time is all that is needed to heal a broken heart, how is it that for some, the wound remains open and any small reminder can trigger the mind to relive the terrible story of the loss, while for others, the torment of not being able to escape the story results in them being engulfed in a never-ending depression with the only way out being to leave this planet to join their loved one?

My ability not only to survive these major tragedies but to thrive, to build up an unwavering resilience, comes from choice. Many years ago, I made a conscious decision to find something positive in every situation, and later on, I chose to find happiness within myself in response to my late daughter's wish from beyond this world. These are not easy choices to make, and I certainly could not have pursued this goal of freedom from pain without the support of family and friends. But credit needs also to be given to my passion for organic gardening and farming, which gave me a life's purpose and a driving force towards action and moving forward. Once I understood that we are all connected, that I was put on this planet to be of service to humanity, my focus changed from one of self-pity and unhappiness to one of joy in helping other people so that they can be healthy and happy too.

Helping others also pleases the ego. You can prove to yourself that you are strong and invincible—a superhero! However, if you have not first worked fully on yourself, then helping others will only be superficial and difficult to sustain. After all, you cannot give what you don't have in the first place. I now know that you need to fill yourself with self-love until it overflows onto others. But at this point in my life story, I evidently still had that lesson to learn.

In the middle of 2015, Stuart dramatically changed jobs without giving his boss any notice. He clearly felt the new position he had been offered was worth upsetting the lady he had been working with for almost four years. Stuart's potential new boss needed him to make a quick decision or else Stuart would have lost the opportunity to travel and make large sums of money. So, despite my warning, Stuart left his employment unceremoniously without looking back. This should have given me a clue as to Stuart's values, but as they say, love is blind.

Stuart had learnt quite a lot about building, and the new job offered further training, in particular on how to put together prefab buildings and add all the finishing touches to complete them. What's more, erecting buildings for Instant Build, his new company, would involve working away from home at various locations in Botswana, such as Kasane and Maun. However, after the first project in Kasane, Stuart told me that the next one would take him and his team much further, across the border to Zambia.

Kasane had taken Stuart away from the farm and me for less than two months, and coming home had not been a very long trip. Zambia was another story, especially as he was commissioned to build clinics in the remote northern parts of the country. Even getting to the villages where the clinics were needed took many hours, due the very poor roads as well as the distance. It was clear from Stuart's communications that he would not be able to return until the work was complete. Not only did this leave me on my own for months on end, but I was left "holding the baby" with all the bills to pay and taking care of our home and animals.

My own business of supplying restaurants and hotels with organically grown vegetables and herbs was doing well. In addition, I was conducting regular workshops for those who wanted to learn how to use the same method of growing. During the cooler months, from March to October, I was also getting an increasing number of school visits, mostly from English medium primary schools. Thus, my teaching skills were helping to supplement the income from the farm produce, and my organisational skills with the monthly farmer's markets at the Eagle's Nest were doing the same. Vegetable sales at the markets and a weekly stall (also at the Eagle's Nest) further added to the money coming in, and I was able to meet all the expenditures without a problem. But there was nothing left for developing the farm or having a short holiday—something I had not been able to afford since the time of the house burning down. Nothing left, that was, until my big surprise on Christmas Day 2015!

My brother Tony called to wish me a merry Christmas but also to tell me about something that would make it even merrier. Through my brother's efforts, we had won a case against the National Health Service in the United Kingdom concerning refunding a portion of the money he'd paid to a private nursing home. Our dear mother had received twenty-four-hour nursing care at the home after she was hit by a major stroke in 2006 until her death in 2009. Tony triumphantly asked me into which bank account I would like the P400,000 deposited!

Stuart automatically thought I would build us a new home like the one we'd had before, but by this time building materials were a lot more expensive, and thus my windfall would not have been enough to build a new house without any input from Stuart. In any case, I no longer had the desire to spend all my money on a big, luxurious house. Once was enough. I now had different priorities in my life. The farm was not only my business; it was a great investment in the future in more ways than one. I wanted to develop the farm further by adding two state-of-the-art tunnels with their own water tank and pump. Then our accommodation needed some improvements, especially the children's bedrooms, which had been partly demolished by termites. And at long last, I could go on holiday!

My plan for a seven-day holiday in the Seychelles was not met with any resistance from Stuart. In fact, he encouraged it. I had been to the Seychelles thirty years before and had always wanted to go back. The last time, I had stayed with a family who had been recommended by a colleague at Sediri Secondary School, but this was to be a "proper" holiday. I was going to stay for a few nights in a bed and breakfast in Mahe (the main island) and then the rest of the time at the expensive resort of St Anne. Stuart was due to start work in a government mine in Lesotho for over three months, from the end of February onwards, and so would not be able to come with me to the Seychelles. But he did not mind his wife going alone. After all, he had already done quite a bit of travelling in his new job, while I had remained behind, taking care of our home.

Regulations for government mines in Lesotho were very strict, and there was a rigorous procedure for entering and leaving the mine. Stuart said he would not be able to come home once he started work in Lesotho, so I should go ahead and have my well-deserved holiday break. I queried why his boss was able to come back to his partner in Botswana at the end of every month if he wasn't, but I was told that Cobus had to come back to pay wages and deal with other business issues.

A few days before I left for my dream holiday, Stuart informed me that he would be home after all—on the day I was flying to Seychelles! He would not arrive until the afternoon, and by then I would be landing on the runway at my destination. I was bewildered as to how Stuart had suddenly gotten permission to leave the mine in Lesotho when I had been told at length how difficult it was do so. The timing was also very strange. Could Stuart not have asked to come home for a few days earlier so that we could spend some time together after all those months away?

My time in the Seychelles was everything I had imagined it would be. At last, I could relax with no long agenda for the day. The first time I sat on the comfortable lounger by the crystal-clear swimming pool with an exotic cocktail by my side, I was overwhelmed with emotion, and tears came to my eyes. *I am finally doing something for myself, demonstrating that I can love me,* I thought. I felt free and light. My troubles disappeared into the blue beyond. It was a wonderful holiday!

I was in for a rude awakening when I got back home. Stuart had already left, which had been his plan, but he had also left the refrigerator empty, using up what he'd found there without replacing it. This made me feel that he didn't care about me, a feeling that was becoming too familiar. Indeed, when Stuart finished his work in Lesotho, he did not rush home to his wife, whom he had not seen for five months. There were evidently people he needed to see more urgently, such as his best friend, his boss, and our neighbours. By the time he finally drove into our yard, he was quite intoxicated, and our reunion was nothing short of a disaster.

While home, Stuart's focus was on his next trip away. He was constantly stressed about his work, and yet it seemed that it was all he was interested in. Getting payment from the various projects was a huge mission, and there were many obstacles in the way of Stuart actually receiving his dues. In the meantime, I continued to single-handedly hold down the fort, making sure all our bills were paid and that we and our animals were fed. On top of this, Stuart showed very little concern for my projects on the farm or the markets that I ran. Although he knew that while he was away, I had to handle everything myself, it did not seem to occur to him that there should be any change during his presence.

It is much easier to pinpoint when the rot set in when you look back after everything has fallen apart. I had accepted being treated with less love than I deserved. After all, I viewed myself as someone unworthy of such love. On occasion, I would become aware that my husband did not show much interest in my appearance, like when I would ask, "How do I look?" as I proudly modelled a brand-new outfit and would receive only a grunt in reply—if I was lucky! Being in the company of loving couples also highlighted for me the fact that something was definitely missing in my own "loving" relationship.

My ability to recognise the positives in the other aspects of my life somehow helped me cope with the negatives in my marriage. As a result, this unhappy state of affairs went on for several years. I tried to have discussions with Stuart concerning his lack of attention to my needs and about my being way down on his list of priorities, but it fell on deaf ears. If any of our friends required assistance, Stuart would drop whatever plans we had and rush to their side, only returning several hours later after several beers had been imbibed. I would talk to Stuart about such issues but not get any response from him, either accepting or denying what I had to say.

In October 2016, shortly after my birthday, I decided I could not stand it anymore. For over a year, there had been no kind of intimacy between us, and I was feeling neglected and unloved. I managed to get Stuart to sit down with me at the garden table, and I poured out my heart. I lamented that there was something very wrong in our marriage and told him that I was extremely unhappy. Stuart just shrugged his shoulders. His only suggestion was that maybe he was going through the effects of midlife crisis, but I was not going to buy that story. Most of our friends were of a similar age, and their marriages were not falling apart.

Stuart eventually conceded that he was not happy either, so I proposed that we get some form of counselling. To my surprise, he agreed, and I quickly asked him who he would like us to see. Stuart did not know of anyone suitable, and when I suggested Alison Bayer, who had helped me heal from Bella's loss, he accepted without any objection. Prior to our first appointment, I found out the cost, and Stuart said he would pay half the fee, which immediately made me feel hopeful that he was serious about repairing our broken relationship.

Sometimes we choose to ignore the truth, particularly if the reality is just too painful for us to accept. At the start of session one, Alison explained that her technique was one of coaching rather than counselling, the difference being that we would come up with our own answers and way forward rather than receiving advice as to what we should do. The very first question that she posed was very pertinent: how did we feel about our relationship? Stuart's answer was immediately exiled to the unreachable depths of my mind.

"I love Lily, but I am not in love with her," he calmly stated.

My answer to the same question was an automatic reflex from the ego to shield myself from pain, but it was not the truth from my soul. "I guess I feel the same," I pretended.

Looking back, Stuart's view of our relationship should have been enough to end the coaching sessions there and then, and indeed to end our marriage. But I refused to examine his straightforward statement. Instead, we continued the session, which concluded with both of us making a commitment to work on certain aspects of our behaviour that we each agreed would help improve our relationship. We would have ten days to carry out these tasks before meeting with Alison again, which would hopefully allow enough time for some progress to be made. Once this was decided, Stuart hastily left to collect his workers and take them home, leaving me and Alison alone in the coaching room. I told my friend that all other aspects of my life were positive and that I hoped that this one would also move in the same direction.

The second session revealed otherwise. Alison asked us how we had fared since the last time the three of us had been together. I stated, in no uncertain terms, that it had been a complete disaster, as far as I was concerned. On the very next evening after the inaugural session, Stuart had done exactly what he had declared that he would not do. He had promised to cut down on his drinking, especially when out with friends, but he had not come straight home from work. Instead, he'd gone to the bar at a nearby restaurant owned by his employers. I'd called after some time to find out his whereabouts and had been told that one of his bosses was retiring and they were having one drink together. Several hours later, a drunken Stuart arrived home. Disappointment did not begin to describe how I felt. I was devastated. If this was an example of Stuart's dedication to saving our marriage, then I might as well throw in the towel. But of course, I did not.

Alison asked Stuart for his side of the story, and he admitted that he was at fault and was sorry for failing to keep to the agreement. After some discussion, I mellowed and conceded that we all make mistakes. Stuart, for his part, said he would make more effort over the weeks to come. It was all I needed to hear, as after all, I still had blinkers on. Even when Alison asked me afterwards how long I was willing to wait for Stuart to change, I did not take that as an indication that she doubted his commitment to healing our relationship.

During the gap between the second and third sessions, I got a glimpse of hope. Stuart walked round the farm with me and showed some interest in the progress I was making with its development. Again, I chose to ignore the fact that I'd had to prompt him several times for this to transpire. The third coaching session involved both Stuart and I taking part in an exercise which required us to fully communicate our feelings. I found this part to be very encouraging, as Stuart was able to talk about his relationship with his mother. I had not heard him express his feelings so openly before. This was to be the last session before the end of the year, but I was confident that we would continue with the exercises that we agreed to complete over the holiday period.

Sadly, my expectation came to nothing. We were both very busy during the first weeks of December. There is always a lot to do before business closes down, so no surprises there. However, just when I thought we would have some time together over the Christmas period, Stuart announced that he was going to Zambia. He had done exactly the same thing the previous year. Stuart spent Christmas Day with Tandy and me and then two days later set off on his travels. His explanation for leaving his family was that this was the best time for him to get the company he was starting in Zambia registered. We were told that unlike in Botswana, the relevant offices would be open in Zambia, and with fewer people around, it would be much quicker to complete the task. Stuart promised he would be back shortly after the new year, as he had done at the start of 2016. This was another promise Stuart did not keep.

At first, I was not unduly worried by the delay in his return, as it was going to be only one or two days and he was communicating with me regularly. Two of his communications took me aback, however, as they were so uncharacteristic of his normal cell phone messages. On one occasion he said "I love you" at the end of our conversation, and in another, he told me that "I have just realised what a wonderful woman you are". I was, of course, pleasantly surprised by these words and tried to just accept them at face value instead of analysing what was behind this sudden show of love.

Then something very terrible happened. The 2-year-old child of Stuart's very close friend was killed by his own mother. Tandy and I went straight to Jeff after he told us the news. The poor man was distraught. Previously, Jeff had been told he could not have children due to the legacy left by the cancer he had suffered some years before. He'd only found out in August 2016 that he had fathered a child, as for some reason, the mother had kept it a secret up until then. Having the little boy in his life had given Jeff a purpose, something to live for, after almost all his family members had passed away due to cancer. This was now such a cruel and painful blow for Stuart's buddy to be dealt.

On the same day, I sent Stuart a text telling him of the tragedy. I described the emotional state of his friend and told him that Jeff needed support to help him cope with the immense grief he was feeling. I expected Stuart's response to be that he would return from Zambia immediately. After all, he had already spent an extra week away from home. However, Stuart replied that he would come back in a day or two. But even that commitment he did not honour, as he only arrived in Botswana the night before the funeral, five days later.

During the funeral, it was Alison and I who stood either side of Jeff, offering both physical and emotional support. Stuart did not come near his friend, except for a few brief minutes, and now that I think of it, he did not come close to me either. It appeared at the time that Stuart did not know how to comfort Jeff, but in hindsight, I have realised that only his body was present at the service—his mind and heart were still in Zambia.

In the days and weeks that followed, there was never a time that was suitable for us to engage in the exercises that we were supposed do together before our next session with Alison. Stuart was running around trying to get quotes he needed for a tender for a school to be built in Gaborone. At least this meant he would be based at home for this job. In addition, Stuart had already agreed that he would take care of both our home and the farm during mid-February, while I was away in India with Tandy on a tour of magnificent gardens. Thus, the coaching exercises were postponed until I was due to return from this historic trip and we would be together again.

Chapter 14

February 2017 is a month I will remember for the rest of my life. The twelve days I spent in India with my daughter were action packed. I had expected to spend the time ambling around the beautiful gardens in the five locations on our itinerary. Instead, we clambered up and down huge staircases, whizzed through narrow passageways, and got to view stunning architecture and many amazing artefacts. Although the tour was organised by *The Gardener* magazine's editor, Tanya Visser, we were shuttled every day to ancient buildings, such as forts, castles, and palaces, including the famous Taj Mahal. The trip was very enjoyable but not exactly what I had envisaged.

It was great to spend some quality time with my daughter after a long period apart. We made new friends with most of the other participants and enjoyed the authentic indigenous cuisine served at some of the hotels and restaurants. I had looked forward to this holiday and break from the farm for many months but was not able to fully relax. Something was not right in my soul, and I could not shake off the feeling that imminent doom was lurking around the corner. I was so much affected that I spent one of the days on my own in our hotel room, recovering from an anxiety attack that had me distraught and fearing that I was going to get palpitations. However, the hotel doctor found nothing wrong with my heart, and I was treated for the cold I had developed.

After losing a day of my holiday to my insecurities, I was determined to enjoy the rest of it. Our time in Agra, with the early-morning visit to the Taj Mahal, put me back on track, as did the evening shopping trip to the street market in New Delhi. The cookery class using Indian spices was also a lot of fun. By the end of the trip, all of our senses had been satisfied, even if we were exhausted. The trip home was a long one, with a several-hours-long stopover in Oliver Tambo airport in Johannesburg. Tandy and I met her boyfriend there, and we passed away some of the time having a lovely lunch together.

During the flight from India to South Africa, I followed the news about the cyclone that had hit Mozambique and was on its way to Botswana. Heavy rain and flooding were predicted, something that Botswana had not experienced for many years. The damage done in Mozambique was very extensive, and I witnessed some of the aftermath on a short holiday there a year afterwards. However, as we got closer to home, the forecast was becoming less daunting, and it seemed that Botswana would be spared similar devastation.

By the time I reached Sir Seretse Khama airport in Botswana's capital city, Gaborone, it was already raining quite heavily. I expected to see Stuart as I emerged through customs control, but he was nowhere to be seen. When I eventually got hold of Stuart on my cell phone, he reported that he had been delayed by having to take his workers home to Oodi, which was in the opposite direction to the airport. I decided to have a glass of wine to try to relax while I waited for him. Although I accepted Stuart's reason for being late, I was disappointed that he was not there waiting eagerly for his wife's return.

The rain seemed to have come to a standstill by the time we got back to the farm, but that was just the calm before the storm. Around 2 a.m., despite being exhausted from my journey, I was awoken by the almost deafening sound of rain on our tin roof. This time it meant business. The torrential rainfall continued unabated and was still pounding our home and farm when we got up in the morning. Our garden was now the thoroughfare for a newly formed river. However, we were not in such a serious predicament as compared to our neighbours, who lived on the edge of Ruretse River at the bottom of our road.

Some of the houses on Combretum Drive were no longer overlooking Ruretse River—they were in it! The water pouring into the river from further upstream had turned it into rapids, bursting the river's banks and even breaking off sections from the Ruretse Dam wall. Stuart and I put on wellington boots and waterproof jackets and drove down Franklin Road as far as the water would allow. Once out of the Pajero, we could see the results of the river's wrath. My first observation was that of the roofs of several vehicles, which were floating in a lake of water. I could not tell what type of vehicles they were, as the rest of each vehicle was completely submerged.

Then, from a distance, I could see a house that appeared to have been reduced to a single-storey building, as the other floor was hidden by the expanded river. One of the families affected had only moved in a month ago; they were busy rescuing their horses and trying to stop their dogs from running amok. Farm workers' houses were also under water, and so their furniture and chickens were being carried to safety. Only the ducks and geese were enjoying the endless pond. I met the owner of the home half under water. She was in shock and had surrendered her emotions. I hugged Lorato and was overwhelmed by my concern for her well-being but also by a growing feeling that all was not well for me either. Apart from the disaster that I could see with my own eyes, I could not shake the one that was lurking somewhere in the shadows of my soul. I felt sure Stuart was hiding a dark secret. Something was very wrong between us.

Only when the rain finally stopped and the river calmed down could the full extent of the damage be assessed. I visited my new friend Lorato several times in the next few days, mostly to offer moral support and cardboard boxes for packing the items from her house that could be salvaged. Some of her family's belongings had been swept away, and one of the refrigerators had been spotted merrily bobbing down the river towards some unknown destination. My visits were also a welcome diversion from what was going on in my own home. I was confused and uneasy about the discoveries which were slowly being unveiled.

I had left frozen meat and ready-to-eat meals in the freezer for Stuart while I was away in India but was surprised to find them still stored there. Other small clues indicated that Stuart had spent very little time at the house while I was gone. Then there were bigger pieces of evidence, such as that the solar geyser had collapsed and lay in pieces on the ground, totally ignored. On one of my trips to town that week, I met a good friend of my mine on the gravel road. We stopped and chatted. I expressed my uneasiness about whether Stuart had really been at home the last two weeks, and she confirmed that I had reason to feel that way. "Oh, yes," she reported, "we met Stuart on the road when he was returning from Zambia!"

The reason it didn't appear that Stuart had spent much time at our home was simple—he hadn't even been in the country. It took one last nail in the coffin of his lies for me to gather up the courage to confront Stuart.

The next morning, I heard my houseworker, Masego, and my farm manager, Samuel, in a heated argument at the kitchen door. I asked Masego to tell me what their problem was. She exclaimed that Samuel had been lying and she was not happy about it. Masego complained that Stuart had left the day after I went to India, and although Samuel had been instructed to feed the animals, he had forgotten to give food to the cats. When she'd arrived in the morning each day, the cats had followed her around, crying from hunger. That is why she was certain Stuart had not been making his bed perfectly every morning and leaving before she got to work, as Samuel had pretended. I was shocked that Stuart could put my chief farmworker in such a position that he had to deceive his own boss, but that was exactly what he had done.

That evening, while we were eating supper at the dining room table, I decided to steer our conversation in a different direction.

"So, did you turn into a vegetarian while I was away, Stuart?" I asked sarcastically. "The meat I left for you is still in the freezer!" Before Stuart could open his mouth, I put forward my own answer that in fact he had not even been sleeping in the house.

"Well, yes, I had to go to Kasane urgently for Cobus," Stuart fumbled.

I pointed out that he had promised to take care of the farm and our animals, so what had happened to that commitment? Furthermore, he was not telling the whole truth, as I knew that he'd gone to Zambia and not just as far as Kasane. Stuart continued to sidestep what really had transpired by admitting that he had just popped over the border to Livingstone as if it were by accident. All that was left was for me to ask him why, in all his text messages, he had not told me of this development. Stuart replied that he had not wanted to spoil my holiday. I calmly concluded, "Well, by blatantly lying to me, you may not have ruined my holiday, but you have definitely done serious damage to our marriage!"

My world came tumbling down. This man had never given me reason to think he was anything other than honest and hard working in our twenty-three years together, but now, I began to wonder what else he was hiding. However, I did not question Stuart further. Already, I was feeling disorientated, and I did not want to end up spinning out of control. The whirlpool in my mind continued to turn as I tried to sleep while in the same bed as the man I had once known. It was not a good night.

In the morning we sat opposite each other at that same table. This time, neither of us felt like eating. Stuart was busy writing a long list of tasks for his day, while I sipped a comforting cup of coffee. Eventually, I decided to speak what was in my tormented heart. "Please add this to your list: 'find accommodation'. I want you to move out by the weekend." Stuart simply nodded in response, packed up his papers, and headed out the door. I watched him go and just felt numb. There was no chance I would call him back. I wanted Stuart out of my sight so that I could lick my wounds in privacy.

Over the next two days, we stayed in the same house but barely spoke. I began to wonder on Friday morning whether Stuart had taken my request seriously, as he had not said anything about moving out. Reluctantly, I asked Stuart, and he reported that Cobus had offered him a room where his mechanics stayed, not far away in Ruretse. He was just left with organising a bed, and then he would move out on Saturday. I confirmed that it was fine and pointed out a few items in the kitchen that he might need before turning my attention to preparing for the market that I was running the next day.

When I returned from the farmer's market at the Eagle's Nest, it was evident that Stuart had kept his word and moved out, taking just a few of his clothes and basic necessities, which was understandable. After all, I had not told him to go for good. I just felt very uncomfortable with him around and needed some space to come to terms with the shock of him lying to me. I had expected him to wait until I got back from town so that we could discuss what he should take, but maybe it was less painful for us both this way. In any case, Stuart sent a message later that he would come on Sunday to finish a job on the farm that he had not yet completed, so I knew we could talk then.

Sure enough, Stuart returned on Sunday afternoon while I was busy doing some transplanting in one of the tunnels. He had brought one of his workers to help move some heavy poles. I went over to see how they were doing, and Stuart asked if he could collect a few more of his things from the house. Naturally, I agreed. However, after they had left and I had finished at the farm, I was shocked with what I found in our bedroom. Stuart had taken every single item that he owned in the room, down to the last scrap of paper! And instead of packing the clothing he would need for a few days, he had simply carted off the chest of drawers in its entirety! This was regardless of the fact that I had paid for it. As far as I can remember, I had asked him to move out temporarily, but it appeared like he was planning on not ever coming back.

On further investigation, I found that Stuart had also taken other items from around the house, in addition to the items I had suggested on Friday. When I told my friend Naledi about this surprising behaviour, she was very concerned and told me that he should not have removed anything from the house without first getting my consent. She advised me to have a meeting with Stuart to state that nothing further should be taken without my approval. With this agenda in mind, I invited Stuart to join me for supper on Tuesday night, which he accepted.

Being in a state of heightened awareness, seemingly trivial events that led to major breakthroughs no longer appeared to me as mere coincidences. Thus, when my cat killed a mouse and left it under the dining room table on Monday night and the corpse was ignored by my houseworker, I was convinced that there was a reason behind it. When I dived under the table to retrieve the lifeless body, I found myself facing a small cardboard box simply labelled "Zambia". I instantly recalled that this was where Stuart had been storing the documents for the company he was trying to register in Zambia. I disposed of the dead rodent and then came back for the box, placing it on top of the table.

Stuart must have forgotten where he had "hidden" the box when removing all his other possessions from the kitchen, dining room, and sitting room. Therefore, the contents of the box were not likely to be of great importance. But somehow, I was compelled to be a "cat" myself and peer inside. My curiosity did not bring forth any rewards at first, but then I noticed that there were a good number of Western Union money transfer receipts. While Stuart may have needed to send some cash to pay the company secretary for her services, there were just too many of the yellow papers. Apart from that, Stuart always claimed to be broke and awaiting payment from the "big bosses", forcing me to pay all our bills in the meantime.

I pulled out one receipt and read it and then another and another. It was not the amount of money that shocked me but who was on the receiving end: "Milly". I knew that Stuart's company secretary was Millicent, and I had previously queried why her name also appeared on the list of directors of his company. He had replied that it was in order to make up the required percentage of Zambian citizens in the directorship. However, the payments were not made to Millicent Inambao but to "Milly", which set off the warning bells in my head. This was why I had been feeling uneasy since I'd returned from India—Stuart was involved with another woman!

Strangely enough, I was comforted by the revelation of Stuart and Milly's relationship. It made sense of the sea of unanswered questions that I had been drowning in. There was still the final step of asking Stuart to confirm my suspicion, but my soul had already certified this conclusion as the truth.

There was no need to look for further evidence; it came to me of its own free will. When I mentioned my discovery to Masego, my houseworker, she was quick to offer her observations that had been bubbling under the surface of her consciousness. She told me about a beautiful necklace she had seen in Stuart's travel bag when he'd come for his short stay while I was in the Seychelles. Masego had expected to see it amongst my jewellery collection, but it had never arrived. She had seen the same fate befall some delicate clothing that appeared when Stuart returned home from Lesotho. It had been in the travel bag but had disappeared as secretly as it had appeared. Such gifts had been destined for someone who Stuart was intimately involved with, and that was certainly not his wife.

All of these findings directed me to seek legal advice. I called up our joint lawyer on Monday morning to make an appointment. I was told that Mr Abdul would only be available on Wednesday afternoon, but I was not concerned, as I was not in any great hurry. I didn't even know quite what I was going to discuss in our meeting, but I was just following the lead from my inner wisdom.

On Tuesday evening, I was cool as the cucumber in the salad I had made as part of our supper. Before we started the meal, I broached the subject that had originally been behind my invitation to Stuart. My requirement that I be informed before anything further was removed from our home was not met with any objection. Indeed, our conversation was relaxed and amicable. Stuart had no idea that he was going to be hit by a ten-pound hammer at any minute.

"So, are you having an affair with Milly?" I glibly asked as Stuart took a mouthful of spaghetti Bolognese. He swallowed and went very pale.

"Ah, well, yes, I was …" was all Stuart could utter.

I continued with the explanation of how I had reached that question, which was really an accusation. Stuart did not try to deny that the money, necklace, and clothing were given to his girlfriend. And then I remembered something else.

"I guess the pregnancy kit I found in the drawer of your bedside table is also hers?"

On this point, Stuart stood his ground that he had been telling the truth when I had first made the discovery nearly a year ago. He still maintained that it had belonged to a friend in Gaborone and that he had sworn to keep her secret. I accepted his answer but told him firmly that in any case, he must have been seeing Milly for at least two years, including during his Christmas visits to Zambia to supposedly get his company off the ground. He did not answer, and he didn't need to either. In my view, the muddy water of the past two years had become crystal clear.

I didn't have a ready-made plan for the way forward but thought I might as well tell Stuart about my appointment with Mr Abdul at 3 p.m. the following afternoon. "You can come along too if you like," I remarked.

Stuart agreed that he would do that as he stood up to leave and make a hasty retreat. Plates may not have been empty, but our supper was definitely over. Stuart said a courteous good night and swiftly drove away. I took the dishes to the sink with the leftovers of our relationship. I already knew in my heart that there was a Grand Canyon between us and that it would be futile to think it could be crossed. So, I chose to think nothing at all, and for the next day, I was simply on autopilot.

I arrived a few minutes before Stuart at the lawyer's office. This gave me the opportunity to give Mr Abdul the background behind the appointed meeting. He listened intently without making any comment. Then, at the same moment as I stated that Stuart would be joining us, he walked through the door. Mr Abdul asked Stuart how things were with him as he sat down in the remaining chair. Stuart explained that he was just about to leave to carry out a major project in Guinea Bissau which would take at least nine months. This was news to my ears, but I was not surprised, seeing that I had been in the dark about so much of what was happening in Stuart's life.

I expected Mr Abdul to probe deeper into what both Stuart and I felt about our situation, but apparently, he had heard enough to draw his own distinct conclusion. Mr Abdul announced, "As I see it, Lily has suffered enough, and the two years that Stuart has more or less been away from home is sufficient grounds for divorce. With Stuart out of the country for the next nine months, the best solution is for Lily to file for irretrievable breakdown of the marriage. Then Stuart does not have to appear in court for the hearings. So, instead of Lily being left in limbo while Stuart is away, she can be free to move on with her life."

The lawyer's statement made perfect sense to us both. There was no need to ask questions, although months later, I did wonder if Stuart had primed Mr Abdul on his vision for the way forward and whether I had been too hasty in agreeing to the suggestion. In just a few minutes, the gates had been flung open to allow our marriage to gallop off into the distance and disappear from sight. My soul did not make any objections to the disappearance. Holding on to our relationship had already caused me great pain, like continuing to grasp a metal object that was glowing hot. Letting go of it was logical for my mind and a sweet surrender for my heart. This time, I did throw in the towel and did it without a tear—it was over!

Chapter 15

One might think that divorce is nothing like losing all your possessions and certainly far from similar to losing a child, and yet in the months that followed, I went through a grieving process. It was still a great loss. I had lost my partner of twenty-three years. And despite it all, I still loved him. Although I instigated the divorce proceedings, it felt like it was my only option and was not a choice I made willingly. After all, Stuart had told Alison and me that he was not in love with me, and it is impossible to make someone love you, no matter how hard you try.

All the emotions that I experienced in my two previous losses were present at different stages during our break-up and beyond. Some were triggered by things Stuart did and said. I felt that he was insensitive to the rawness of my wounds from the hurt he had caused, which brought up feelings of anger and a desire for revenge, while at other times, I concluded that I somehow deserved his betrayal due to not showing him enough appreciation and love. Maybe I had been too controlling and "bossy", as one of our friends recalled Stuart describing me. Again, I wondered why I hadn't seen it coming, just like Bella's death. But of course I didn't see it, because I had no reason to distrust the man who had shown me, as well as all his friends, so much loyalty. Stuart was a straightforward, honest guy—everyone knew that!

I did not shed many tears as we went on our separate paths but rather felt an underlying sadness and loneliness. I had gotten used to being on my own and thus being *alone* during the months on end when Stuart had been working away from home, but this was not the same as being *lonely*. I was quite capable of running the farm and my business without his help, but there was a big hole in my life. There was no longer the anticipation of Stuart returning home at the end of a work project. There was no longer a need to plan things together or to organise appointments for him. There was only person left to take care of and to love now—me, myself, and I—and looking back now, that was exactly what I'd needed to do! Ultimately, the divorce from Stuart had resulted in this important realisation. Thus, not only could I forgive him, but I could also be grateful for the role he'd played in my life.

Putting myself first was not something that I was accustomed to doing, but I was determined to stop anyone from raining on my parade again. I decided that I was going to emerge from this third major trauma and loss not just stronger but totally independent. And yet, try as I might to achieve this new aim, I still felt I needed someone to complete my happiness equation. I needed someone to tell me that I am beautiful, that I am a wonderful woman, that I am loved.

Soon after the divorce was through, I was on the lookout for a companion. Then I met someone who was young and handsome and who said sweet things to me. He did not have a well-paying job and said that phoning me was not easy for him. I found myself calling him every night until I suddenly woke up to the fact that I was the only one making an effort in our relationship. Instead of feeling better about myself, I felt the opposite. I was clearly not on the right path to loving myself more.

The next plan of action was to forget meeting anyone and concentrate solely on making myself happy. I was no longer in any hurry to meet someone, and I had plenty to keep me occupied, with the approaching Christmas markets and keeping the farm going despite the challenges of El Nino and climate change. However, I did join a series of Let Him Find You webinars, just for fun more than anything else. I carried out the exercises at the end of each session, and one of them was to list all the qualities that I would want in the soulmate of my dreams. The idea was that you need to know what you are looking for before you can recognise it when it stares at you squarely in the face.

Then out of the blue, just when I felt that I was content with being single, the Universe decided otherwise. Maybe it was because

I was happy with my new status that I was in a position to attract someone else. I was no longer "wanting". I was enjoying my life and loving myself just as I was, with all my perfect imperfections! When Ruby, the floor manager at Star Cafe, uttered the words "Girl, has that guy got his eyes into you!" I wanted to run and hide. Eventually, I had no choice but to turn around and pass my admirer in order to get out of the restaurant. Our eyes met, and I was almost trapped in a cage of emotion. I surrendered a polite greeting and swiftly made my escape through the open door.

When I returned two days later to do the delivery of mixed lettuce and herbs, Ruby told me that this engaging young man with the big brown eyes had requested my phone number. Although my mind told me that this was the last thing I should do, my heart pulled me over to where he was standing. By then, I knew his name. It was a name that presaged the role he would have in my life—Daliso. On receiving my phone number, he politely asked when would be a good time for him to call. This man was a gentleman. He made a good impression on my soul from the start, and every day, I ticked off more of the qualities from the homework list that I had written some weeks before.

Three years later, Daliso and I are still together. I can safely say that I have never felt so at peace and secure in my being. Not only do I have an amazing man in my life who continually reminds me of how much he loves me, but I am surrounded by an ever-increasing network of loving and supportive friends. I have been told that I have *too many* friends and that people can only have a few *real* friends, but I have never believed these limitations to be true. In my book, there is no limit to love, so why should the number of people you love and those who love you be restricted? After all, we are the ones who construct those restrictions. Love and friendship are fundamental to happiness.

Another essential contributor to being in a state of happiness is having gratitude. I have carried out several gratitude programs, such as documenting ten things that I am grateful for each day in a journal for a period of twenty-eight days. I am also a member a gratitude group on Facebook that is the brainchild of Jean Harvey, who left Botswana to return to her home in the United Kingdom. The initial premise was for the members to post five things they were thankful for on the page, again each day for a month. However, group members found it such a valuable exercise that it was followed by a 100-day stint of gratitude, and the page continues to be actively supported as I finish writing this book.

Finally, I cannot stress enough the importance that forgiveness has played in bringing happiness into my life. In forgiving what I have done to myself and what I perceived other people to have done to me, it has enabled me to let go of the past. That albatross flies free, and so does my soul. I have learnt that by harbouring resentment, hatred, anger, and bitterness, I left little space for healing and real joy in my heart. Each time I made the choice to forgive various players in my life's journey, my heart instantly felt lighter, and positive energy could flow through me with much greater ease.

Together, love, gratitude, and forgiveness are the tools that we can use to create joy within, and in turn, they manifest as a beautiful life on the outside. We are all much more powerful than we choose to acknowledge. In Marianne Williamson's book A Return to Love, she makes the famous statement, "our deepest fear is not that we are inadequate. Our deepest fear is that we are powerful beyond measure ….." Each one of us has a role to play in transforming this world into a better place so that we leave a legacy of love for future generations. We can all grow happiness!

Afterword

COVID-19 Takes Over the World (written in May 2020)

Life is full of surprises, some good, some not so good. When I started writing this book about the challenges I had experienced in the past, I had no idea that by the time I would finish it, we would be in the middle of a global pandemic. At the start of 2020, I was full of excitement at what I thought was going to be a year of abundance—"twenty plenty", as I repeated to all my friends. And then, a few months later in April, over a million people had contracted the novel virus COVID-19, and many thousands had died across the world. Wuhan, a city in China, was hit first, followed by Italy, Spain, Germany, Iran, the UK, and the USA, to name a few of the badly affected countries. As I write, the country where I live, Botswana, has just thirteen cases with only one death but has joined many countries in going into a complete lockdown where most people are not allowed to leave their houses except for food and medical supplies.

At first, I was anxious and scared as the news spread, with an avalanche of information tumbling on top of us from governments, the television, and more, especially from the many forms of social media. A lot of it has been doom and gloom, with only predictions that the situation will get worse and we'll have many months ahead of being in this state of emergency. Like everyone else, I was checking myself to see if I displayed any of the recognised symptoms and would start panicking if I my throat showed any signs of soreness. Following the protocols to avoid picking up the virus at least gave me some sense of order and control, but there was still this underlying feeling of "what is going to happen next?" Then there was the feeling of overwhelming sadness at all the people who were sick and suffering, those whose loved ones were dying but who they could not say goodbye to, those who had lost loved ones, those who were vulnerable and alone, and those who were on the frontline, putting themselves at so much risk. It was certainly very difficult to find anything to be happy about.

Caroline Myss believes that the COVID-19 pandemic had to happen to avoid a far worse catastrophe, such as a Third World War, which at the time the pandemic started was a tinder box just waiting to be lit. To prevent the spread of the virus, countries will have to work together, not against each other. As we slowly come out of lockdown and borders open again, there needs to be much discussion between governments on how this will be done in a controlled manner. I don't think there is any country whose economy which has not been severely affected by the restrictions. The money we might spend on war preparations is urgently needed to help those who have lost their jobs, those who cannot pay their rent, and those who are unable to feed their families. All attention should be shifted towards recovery from this disaster. Just as it is a time for individuals to reflect on what is truly valuable in their lives and thus what they should spend their time and other resources on, it is time for the leaders of our world to do the same.

Building Up Resilience through Adversity

Eckhart Tolle declares that "life has to become difficult for evolution to happen." When I think of how animal species have changed over the years, it is clear to me that they did not just wake up one day and decide to change. Changes had to happen for species to survive instead of becoming extinct. Some were more successful than others. Evolution is not spontaneous; it occurs as a result of a catalyst. A driving force which alerts the species that a change is imperative. For individuals and humanity as a whole to grow and evolve, it seems that we must have some form of major adversity to be the precursor to that awakening. Adversity, according to Tolle, forces us to develop greater strength and consciousness. In other words, *per ardua ad astra*, which is a Latin phrase meaning "through adversity to the stars". Awakening does not usually happen in your comfort zone, states Tolle, but rather when there is disorder.

So, during this time of adversity, I turned my focus inward to where I could do something instead of feeling helpless and hopeless. What I found inside was an array of tools that I had built up over the years and could now use in the present challenging situation.

I had gone through major economic loss when my house burnt down and for several years had relied on handouts and the generosity of others, and yet I was now in the possession of a flourishing farm and a range of different income avenues. In April 2020, those avenues came to an abrupt halt. The restaurants and hotels that the farm supplied were closed. The markets were not allowed to operate. The people who regularly bought my vegetables and herbs could no longer buy them. My workshops were mostly postponed indefinitely, and visits by school children were out of the question. But I got my creativity and resilience out from the toolbox and started inventing new ways of getting my produce to people and making an income using the modern technology which had suddenly become my best friend instead of being something from the unknown.

Another very useful tool was the one of health care. With my heart condition having once threatened my very existence, I had adopted a fairly healthy lifestyle and good eating habits that sustained and nurtured my body instead of putting it under stress. This, I believe, has helped to build up my immune system. When everything started, I was already at the stage where I hardly fell prey to a cold, let alone any other illness. By maintaining and building on this healthy way of living, surely I would not let the dreaded virus get the better of me!

Going through loss, especially that of my daughter, and coming out of the other end gave me the clear knowledge that this too shall pass. In this book, I have talked about how my determination to survive the major traumas in my life represents the phoenix rising out of the fire. Caroline Myss uses a similar analogy about "riding the phoenix". She states that there is a "divine holy promise" that no matter how much we lose, we always get our lives back. The cycle of loss is inevitable, but the sacred promise is that we will rise. We will always rise from the ashes. Thus, we need to surrender to that ride instead of stressing as to whether we are going to get through the pandemic or not.

> *Let us help the phoenix to rise from the ashes; let us help lay the foundation for a new renaissance; let us help to accelerate the spiritual awakening until it lifts us into the golden age which would come.*
>
> —*Peace Pilgrim*

As I put the finishing touches to this afterword, the Universe decided to give me one final test of my resilience. Two days ago, the news reached me that Bella's killer is to be released from prison in October this year, having barely served half of his fifteen-year sentence. My other daughter, Thandiwe, is understandably outraged and tells me that she is going to make it known that this is not acceptable. But I have searched in my toolbox and found that I have already used forgiveness to set me free from the atrocity that this young man committed. I have let go of the anger and hurt. I have no need for hatred or revenge. I am at peace. Happiness continues to grow in the garden of my life.

To find out how you can grow happiness organically, and to get your free guide on Preparing Vegetable Beds please send an email to growinghappiness888@gmail.com just stating 'Veg Beds'. Thank you.

Printed in the United States
by Baker & Taylor Publisher Services